Praise for *And Now, Back to*

"Rita Lussier's *And Now, Back to Me* is a
the empty nest: marriage, kids, career, aging parents, and the warm
embrace of community."

—Matt Bombeck, writer and son of Erma Bombeck

"As someone who recently became an empty nester and is approaching retirement, I so appreciated reading about Rita's journey through this challenging but invigorating time of life. Rita shows us how responsibilities will change, relationships will shift, and opportunities will emerge, and she points out that we need to be prepared to be kind to ourselves as we navigate this uncharted territory. So much of what she shares resonates with my own experiences. Her insights helped me to face the future with optimism."

—Cynthia Dawson Bonn, Dean of Admission,
The University of Rhode Island

"*And Now, Back to Me* made me laugh, cry and most of all relate. This beautifully written memoir is a collection of essays that tell the story of every woman—or at least many of us—who combine career and family. It explores the mixed joy of reclaiming independence when the last child leaves the house and the ache of taking care of aging parents, all with honesty, insight and tenderness. A great read and a great gift for so many women you know."

—Jan Brogan, author of *The Combat Zone*

"It feels like Rita has taken the hand of every mother, to reassure us that even when our kids are fully grown, we get to keep growing too."

—Liz Gumbinner, writer, creative director, and former
editor-in-chief of Cool Mom Picks

"Rita Lussier's poignant memoir offers a revealing, intimate look into life's crossroads moments and the choices that define us. It's a captivating read about the power of shaping the life you desire. With emotional honesty and reflection, she takes the reader on a journey of the heart."

—Teri Rizvi, director of the Erma Bombeck Writers' Workshop and author of *One Heart with Courage: Essays and Stories*

"*And Now, Back to Me* will resonate with any woman experiencing the many changes that come with our midlife stretch—the pull of children and partners, aging parents, society, and our expectations of ourselves. Through beautiful, authentic, and occasionally melancholic vignettes, Ms. Lussier encourages us to find joy in the everyday moments, in those around us, and especially in our own journeys, past, present, and future."

—Amy Baumgartel Singer, Director of College Counseling, The Wheeler School, Providence, Rhode Island

"Just in time for my emptying nest, *And Now, Back to Me* inspired with its wit, optimism, and wisdom. While anyone might enjoy Rita Lussier's collection of stories, they are especially meaningful for those contending with the empty nest, aging bodies, ailing parents, and, perhaps, having more time on our hands. These personal stories invite us to get to know ourselves in new ways, reinvent our lives and careers, and choose how we spend our time in the meaningful next stage of life."

—Lisa Tener, author of Stevie Award winner *Breathe. Write. Breathe.: 18 Energizing Practices to Spark Your Writing and Free Your Voice*

And Now, Back to Me

And Now, Back to Me

Stories from an Empty Nest

Rita Lussier

SHE WRITES PRESS

Published 2025
Printed in the United States of America
Print ISBN: 978-1-64742-770-2
E-ISBN: 978-1-64742-771-9
Library of Congress Control Number: 2024919412

For information, address:
She Writes Press
1569 Solano Ave #546
Berkeley, CA 94707

Interior Design by Kiran Spees

She Writes Press is a division of SparkPoint Studio, LLC.

For Elaine and André
for always believing.
In God.
In love.
In me.

A very important thing is not to make up your mind that you are any one thing.

—Gertrude Stein

Contents

And Now, Back to Me

Four days into my dream job at an advertising agency in Providence, Rhode Island, I discovered what I'd really be doing for the next three decades. The lunchtime appointment would be just a quick walk around the corner to the clinic. The encounter would be awkward. That I knew. But I could endure anything in return for the peace of mind I'd feel once the ordeal was over.

From out of my purse, I took the little jelly jar I'd wrapped in a plastic bag to keep its contents—my first-morning urine—from leaking. I lowered my eyes and handed it to the woman at the desk. The transaction seemed common enough. Dozens of young, anxious women came here every day. I was just another name on the appointment list. Nothing more. That's what I told myself as I sat in the waiting room, apprehensively thumbing through an old issue of *People*.

I was not alone. A young woman wrapped in a cozy sweater sat on the other side of the table where the magazines fanned out in a spread of unlikely distractions. She looked over and smiled. "This is my third time here. Hopefully, it's a charm."

I managed a weak nod in her direction. Then they called my name. I walked into the inner office and stood in front of another woman behind another desk, shifting back and forth in my new suit and heels until she motioned for me to sit in one of the wooden chairs. I stared at the clock on the wall, noting I'd be late returning to work.

And then, there it was. Just like that. The news rumbled out of her mouth like rolling thunder: *Pregnant!*

In that one short moment, my life divided into two distinct parts. The first, when nearly everything was about me. The second, when almost nothing was. I wasn't ready.

Didn't matter. Sometimes, a power greater than us knows more about who we are, what we need, and where we belong than we could ever imagine, plan, or orchestrate. As reluctant as I was, as accidentally as it happened, motherhood fit me perfectly.

Perhaps you know the feeling. Unexpectedly, something turns your head around, and it just feels right. A new job you almost didn't accept. A friend you meet who seems to know what you're going to say even before you do. A lover's first embrace, which throws you off balance, and suddenly you're falling, falling, falling. For me, it was tiny fingers grasping my hand so tightly that I felt a tug inside. A shift in my soul. An awakening that someone needed me in a greater way. And just like that, I was home. I was *creating* a home. This was where I belonged. Where we belonged.

Two kids, two marriages, and more than two career changes later, just as that first visit to the clinic had ushered in sudden and unforeseeable change, another moment would ring in yet another transition for me. This time, however, I knew it was coming. In fact, I'd been preparing for the inevitable day for years.

As it turned out, my preparations didn't account for Hurricane Irene, the power outage, the last-minute packing by flashlight, the anything-that-didn't-need-to-be-heated dinner of leftover pizza and Cheerios, all adding to the tension my husband, Ernie, and I were already feeling the night before driving our youngest child, Meredith, to New York University for the first time. But the next morning, the skies brightened, and we climbed into our car as planned, jammed to the hilt with boxes, bags, and nervous excitement.

On the sidewalk in front of her dorm, the day had turned sunny and warm, with a few fallen branches on Twelfth Street the only evidence of a storm. But the morning was anything but quiet. Students in bright blue T-shirts rolled big carts in every direction, talking and laughing as they greeted freshmen and their families, helping to unload all their belongings and ushering them into their new residence.

Once inside Room 3C, we met Meredith's roommate and her mother, the two of them busy unpacking and organizing. We pitched in, making beds and new acquaintances until a knock on the door summoned the two freshmen to a welcome-to-the-dorm meeting. After a few hugs, while we moms held back more than a few tears, our girls took off chattering down the hallway, leaving us with nothing to do but walk away.

Ernie reached over and took my hand as we made our way to the parking garage and the 180 miles or so of highway that seemed so different than it had just a few hours before.

"Everything went well," I said as we settled into our car and headed north toward our home in Jamestown, Rhode Island.

"Her roommate was nice," Ernie said.

"Meredith seemed happy."

"Hope we hear from her later."

"Me, too."

As the miles rolled on, the conversation drifted off. Maybe all the packing and the unpacking, the storm, and the uncertainty had taken their toll. Maybe we were tired. Or maybe we just didn't know what to say after our youngest child was no longer tethered to our day-to-day comings and goings, her tenuous orbit suddenly ripped free from our watchful eyes. The silence between us was unexpected, but after all, this was uncharted territory. Not to worry. We'd figure it all out once we got home to what some might call *an empty nest*.

Some. But not me.

⸛

I open the door and realize our home is not empty after all. I am here. Ernie is here. So is our faithful, albeit somewhat crazy, black Labrador, Lizzie. And although I suspect it will take me—and us—a little time and more than a little struggle and introspection to reshape this new life, I'm looking forward to the next part of our journey.

As it turns out, the woman who couldn't quite accept the news at the clinic all those years ago, the mother who had no idea that bringing children into the world would bring *her* out into the world in new and unimaginable ways, the career-focused professional who never envisioned that raising kids would also raise her consciousness—that woman is capable of yet another monumental and wondrous shift in her life. At least, I think I am.

And now, back to me.

Up and Running

Stretch out the right leg. Push it up against the tree. Cinch the shoelaces tight and secure. Left leg, same drill. Ready? Doesn't matter. Just go. Down the driveway, turn right, and head out. Past neighbors walking their dogs in the early morning chill. Past rows of recycling bins ready for pickup at the edge of the road. Past kids and parents waiting for the school bus to arrive.

I used to wait there. Not anymore.

Don't stop. Don't think.

It's okay not to think. That's what I tell myself. Just run past the confusion clogging my head. My muddled thoughts will settle into a rhythm once my feet do. I should know this by now. I've been running since college, ever since I found the pathway to losing the chubbiness that shaped my girlhood, and not in a pleasant way. Over time, running became more to me than a way to keep fit. My early morning run has become a ritual, my meditation, my centering practice. Before I join the rest of the world, I can be alone with my thoughts and feelings. I can sort out my schedule for the day, wrestle with doubt or fear, and come to the finish line in better shape than I started. Running changed me. It strengthened my body, my mind, and my spirit.

I could use some strength now.

For twenty-seven years, my mission had always been clear.

Didn't matter that I had stumbled onto it without all the planning and consideration that had gone into selecting which courses to study in college and graduate school, which positions I'd pursue in marketing and advertising, how to run the consulting business I created with my friend Joyce, or which topics I'd cover in the newspaper column I wrote for a dozen years. I had chosen those steps in my life in a careful, calculated manner. But this mission seemed to have chosen me.

Unlike my career, I had not prepared for motherhood. Growing up in the sixties and seventies, I had passed up the traditional home economics and child development courses, preferring to explore subjects like political science and management—anything empowering me to take advantage of the exciting new possibilities opening up for women. In much the same way, I grew up enthusiastically following all the accomplishments of my father's career as Bandmaster in the Navy while paying little mind to the sacrifices my mother made in keeping our home and family together while he traveled all over the globe. All I knew was that I wanted a different kind of life than hers; one in which I made my own money, my own success, and maybe even a difference in the world.

On a sunny October day nearly eight months after that awkward visit to the clinic, the mission began. Geoff was born, and I became enamored with an impossibly tiny and perfect human being. Unexpectedly, I found myself falling into a new kind of love, primal and fierce, taking me to places I'd never imagined.

My bathroom, for example.

Geoff was two at the time, with a tousle of red curls and an impish grin. In the tiny house in Newport, Rhode Island, where we were living after his father and I separated, I got locked in the bathroom. Not sure how it happened, although I have a small theory. My only hope of escape was convincing the toddler in the hallway laughing at my predicament to slip the key under the door. Eventually, he did.

When I wasn't commuting or working at the advertising agency, Geoff and I were inseparable. On spring evenings, we'd walk to the nearby convenience store, playing a game of kicking the same pebble all the way there and then all the way home. On weekends, we'd hike to the beach, ride around Ocean Drive on my bicycle, or play in the neighborhood park until the sun slipped away from us.

I had little time to mourn the end of my marriage with my little prankster by my side. There was the night an odd, spicy aroma drifted into my dreams, and I woke to find the prankster sitting on my bed cross-legged in footed pajamas, grinning while chewing on a stick of pepperoni, the same one that had been forbidden earlier in the evening. When I came home from work on another day, I wondered why all the older neighborhood boys had gathered outside Geoff's bedroom window. Might have had something to do with the dollar bills he handed them. The ones that had come from my wallet! And on more than one morning, as I headed bleary-eyed into the bathroom to get ready for work, I switched on the light and shrieked. Who would have expected to see a giant, overstuffed bear perched on the toilet seat? During those days, Geoff kept me on my parenting toes for sure, and on more level footing than I might have found on my own.

So when the man I had been dating seemed to be getting more serious about our relationship, perhaps you can understand why I hesitated. I had just dug myself out of a deep, dark, and ugly hole with my own hands, on my own terms, fashioning a fairly smooth and content life for my son and me in our little house. Why, then, would I take a risk that could easily have catapulted me back into the abyss? Even worse, Geoff could fall in there with me. I'd come too far from abandonment and learned that the best person to trust was me. I'd worked too hard to let myself believe again in white lace and promises or happily ever after. And yet, I wanted to.

And then came the night at the sports bar. Ernie and I slid into a booth and ordered two beers and a platter of nachos. I found myself chattering to fill in the silence. "So, how about those Celtics?" "Can you believe how windy it is?" "Tom Hanks, you gotta love the guy." Nothing I said warmed him up.

Then in a flash, he pulled a tiny box from his pocket. He placed it gingerly on the table in front of me without saying a word. For a moment, I hesitated. I looked around; a basketball game blared on the phalanx of television sets strategically placed throughout the smoky room. I glanced down at the salsa-stained faded jeans and smiled. Sometimes, life catches you when you least expect it.

Crossroad moments are often like that. They knock us off our feet without warning. No instructions tucked inside the box. No directions to turn right, then left, and arrive safely at our destination. Our heads scream, *No! Get up and run! We've been hurt before. This won't be any different. He won't be any different.* Yet, we hesitate. Something deeper inside wants us to believe. Needs us to believe. Again. Just one more time. One more chance at magic. One more chance to fly. Maybe this time it will work out. Maybe we will fit together. Tightly, sweetly, and forever.

The next morning, I pulled the tiny box out of my purse and showed Geoff the ring. The look of doubt on my face must have been wildly evident, even to a five-year old.

"Mom, do you love him?"

"Yes."

"Then you should marry him."

Do you love him?

Geoff's question brought me to the essence of things and eventually across the Newport Bridge and over Narragansett Bay from our little house to the one in Jamestown where Ernie waited for us. The same one in the same neighborhood where I'm running past all these memories.

Not long after we settled into our new house, our family of three became four as we welcomed Meredith, another even more impossibly tiny human. With an infant and an eight-year-old, with one hand rocking the cradle and one foot kicking a soccer ball, time just seemed to speed up.

Some mornings, I'd tuck our little auburn-haired baby into her car seat and drive Geoff to school. Sometimes, Ernie came along, and we'd stop to pick up coffee and muffins, one of the perks of running our own businesses from out of our home. On those rides around the island of Jamestown, I tried to freeze frame the scenes of rocky coastline and grassy marshes and rows of pine trees that flashed by outside my window, locking them into my memory just in case I ever needed proof that changing my life, moving from there to here was possible. Not easy. But possible.

One particular Saturday, our morning jaunt took us over the bridge to Newport to our favorite café for breakfast. Our toddler could not stay seated for scrambled eggs or buttered toast, what with all the rhythmic reverberations coming from the dance class on the second floor. "I want to do that," Meredith said, her tiny feet tapping, her hazel eyes flashing with determination. A call to Miss Miki, the studio's artistic director, told us what we needed to know. As soon as Meredith was out of diapers, she could start. And she did! Beginning ballet was just that: the beginning of friends, performances, and a centering routine for her young life.

I mentioned that she's determined. Add to that, persistent. Every December, Meredith wrote the same letter despite not getting an answer:

*Dear Santa, please bring me a puppy. Please, please, please!
I've been extra good this year. I want a black Labrador. I promise I will take care of it. Love, Meredith.*

After years of hoping, praying, and—most of all—believing, Santa
came through, although he waited until the summer when she was
eight. That's when Lizzie, the black Labrador of all those Christmas
wishes, came true—leaping, bounding, licking, and chewing her way
into our lives. So many times, we all walked together around this
very neighborhood where I'm now running, Lizzie stopping to sniff
at every rock, twig, and patch of grass.

Despite the demands coming from so many directions, our little
blended family and our puppy grew—even thrived. Days raced into
nights, weeks blurred into months, and then years. Ernie and I were
two parents, not unlike others, shuttling from business meetings
to client presentations, from play dates to school plays, from tennis
matches to ballet recitals, from family gatherings to holiday parties,
trying to hold on to the moments, as if staying in the busy flow of
things could stop the inevitable when one day Geoff would pack
up his books, clothes, and computer, and we would drive him to
George Washington University, and on the very long trip home from
Washington, DC, there would be just three of us sitting in the car left
to wonder what had just happened.

It would happen again.

Meredith's love of dancing and performing led her to acting, and
her persistence and determination led her to insist on auditioning for
acting programs at colleges despite her high school guidance coun-
selor warning us of the long odds. But odds are just numbers that
don't always predict dreams, and Meredith's led her to painting her

toenails by flashlight so she could put her best foot forward at NYU the next morning. Despite Hurricane Irene. Despite the long odds.

And I'm trying to put my best foot forward here as well, running, thinking, and running some more.

How did I get here so quickly? How is it possible that I'm on the same road, passing the same trees, the same houses, the same faces, and yet, as I turn into my driveway, nothing feels the same, nothing seems to fit anymore?

"Hey, Rita," my neighbor, June, calls from across the street. "Did you make it to New York?"

"We did. We got Meredith all settled into her dorm. What a big transition!"

"I bet."

"The house feels so different."

"You'll get used to it."

"I hope you're right. Have a good day."

As I climb the stairs to my house, I can't help wondering why I feel so lost, so empty. It's the same run, same neighborhood, and same house, but the feeling is as foreign as a distant country.

I'd known this change was coming. For months, I'd been looking forward to having more time to myself for rebuilding my career, reenergizing my marriage, visiting my parents, planning for retirement, catching up with friends, and maybe even renovating our house. But ever since we got back from New York, I just don't have the energy. I can't seem to find the inspiration.

But today will be different.

It's a new dawn.

And I am up.

And I am running.

First Weekend Alone

The narrow street outside the yoga studio in Newport is home to two restaurants, a bank, and several office buildings. During the tourist season, parking spots are hard to come by, and if you're lucky enough to find one, you'll need a pocketful of quarters to feed the meters. But when my Friday evening class is over, his car will be out there waiting for me. This I know.

What I don't know is what we're doing.

"Why don't we go out to dinner?" Ernie suggests as I slide into the passenger seat and close the door.

"I'm in my leggings and still sweating. Not sure I'm dressed for it."

"You want to go home then?"

"Seems like we should do something."

"What are you thinking?"

"I don't have any ideas."

Ernie takes a left turn away from the bridge that would take us home and keeps driving with no apparent destination in mind. The purring engine and my growling stomach make me keenly aware of the silence in the car.

Silence in the car is a new thing. When one kid or the other or both were along for the ride, quiet was unthinkable. If it was just Ernie and I out running errands, we usually had so much pent-up news to catch up on between us. Work. The kids. Running the house and our businesses. Parents, friends, and neighbors. There never seemed to be enough miles to carry us through all we had to say.

But here we are in the empty nest where everything is changing. Take one piece out and try putting the puzzle back together; it just doesn't fit in the same way. We parents get so fixated on what it will be like for our kids to go off into the world, what we'll feel like when we open the door and see an empty bedroom, that we don't anticipate some of the other repercussions we'll face. Like redefining our marriages, for better or worse, all over again.

"How about Mama Leone's?" Ernie says after winding up and down streets lined with historic houses on the scenic point overlooking Narragansett Bay. "We can get a glass of wine, order takeout."

Relieved to have some direction, we head to the nearby restaurant, which is owned by neighbors who, over the years, have become our friends. We pull two seats up to the bar and settle in. Strange, but it feels as though we're on a first date. In some ways, maybe we are.

Joanna comes over and greets us. It's hard to hear her with the buzz of conversation all around and the Red Sox game blaring on all the TVs. "Look at the lovely couple out on a Friday evening," she says, pouring us a glass of chardonnay and a draft beer. "What brings you two out tonight?"

"You're not going to believe this," I say leaning over the bar and smiling at our pretty neighbor, her long, shiny hair tied high in a ponytail that bounces up and down as she moves. "This is our first weekend alone."

"Since when?"

"Since ever. When we got married, we already had Geoff. And now that Meredith is off at college, this being alone thing is a whole new adventure."

"Hey, neighbors!" Matt says as he pulls up a stool next to me. He tells us he just got off his shift at the hospital, and while he's waiting for the pizza he ordered to take home, he's got time for a beer.

"We were just telling Joanna that this is our first weekend alone. We took Meredith to NYU last week and here we are, just the two of us," I tell him.

"I'll drink to that!" Matt laughs and holds up his glass. He's still got a son and a daughter at home, and he tells us his parents are staying with him at the moment.

An older couple settles into the empty seats next to Ernie and introduces themselves. Apparently, Paul and Linda have been camping near the beach, and they've come in for a good hot meal and the chance to watch the game.

"Looks like they're headed to the playoffs this year," Paul says as Ernie and I look at the menu.

"Why don't you stay for dinner?" Joanna asks as she pours more wine and beer.

"I think we'll just get takeout," Ernie says and orders us a Caesar salad and a pepperoni pizza. "We need to get home and let Lizzie out. She gets restless when we leave her alone for too long."

After another inning or so, our order is ready. We pay our tab, then gather our box and our bag while wishing our friends a good night.

"What do you want to do this weekend?" Ernie asks as he heads for the Newport Bridge and the scenic two-mile journey that takes us home over the bay.

"Seems like we should do something."

"What are you thinking?"

"I don't have any ideas. "

We drive along in a silence that feels oddly comfortable this time around, and a relaxed sensation settles into my bones. Maybe it's the yoga, the wine, or the giddy sense of freedom in the air. Maybe it's all of the above.

"How about I get up early tomorrow and run into town?" I suggest after a while. "You could meet me there. We'll go for coffee."

"Sounds like a plan."

Maybe not a plan, but it's a start. The beginning of what will hopefully lead us to the next thing, whatever it may be. Who knows? Who knows anything at this point?

Well, there is *one thing*. When tomorrow comes, and my run into town is over, his car will be out there waiting for me. This I know.

But will it be enough?

Got Questions? Ask a Horse.

"So you've got no idea where you're going?" Ernie asks as I scramble around our bedroom, pulling on jeans and a sweater in the dawning light that tells me it's way too early to be up on a Saturday.

"All she said was to dress warmly in layers and be ready at 7:30. I wish I had time to make coffee. I hate not knowing where I'm going."

"Relax. Carol's your best friend. She's probably got a plan to help you. She knows you've been struggling ever since Meredith left for college."

As we set out in her car, the sun no match for the autumn chill, Carol grins when I ask where we're going. "Just sit back and take it easy for a change. My GPS knows exactly where we're going."

I look over at my friend. Her blond hair is tied back in a ponytail and a sly smile reveals how much she's enjoying keeping the surprise to herself. This is just another of the many adventures we've shared since we met in fourth grade. How lucky I am that she's taking time out of her weekend to help me figure things out.

She's good at that. She gets me. She knows every bit of my history—the good, the bad, and the ugly— and she's loved me through it all. That's why, on the devastating morning all those years ago when I got fired from my job at the second advertising agency I worked at in Providence, I headed straight for her office. I burst in and explained, with tears and mascara streaming down my face, that my bosses had asked me to meet them at some men's club. I told her how great I was at my job and how they'd tried making me think otherwise during the meeting, but when I broke down sobbing, they somehow softened and admitted they were firing me because I was dating Ernie, their partner. I went on to tell Carol, while crying, sighing, and blowing my nose, that I only had enough money for Geoff and me to live in the tiny house in Newport for four months, and I felt shaky, and frightened, and had no idea what to do. She listened to all of it, never moving her gaze from me except when she got up for a box of Kleenex. "This could be good," was what she said when I was done. *This could be good.* I couldn't see it at the time, but Carol did.

Now steering us down a bumpy road she asks, "So what are you thinking? Did you take that offer from the *Journal?*"

"It was so hard to decide, Carol. You know how much I loved writing my column. After all the years I spent in advertising and marketing, the newspaper was the first job I ever truly connected with. It forced me to tell the truth about my life, to make sense of little moments and big occasions. Of course, it helped that Ernie was making most of the money and I was free to focus on the kids and the column."

"What happened?"

"There was an editorial shakeup. The new editor wanted me to write something different for the Sunday paper. But I wasn't sure. There were so many creative restrictions, and after nearly twelve years of the column, I thought it was a good time to move on. To what, I don't know. But I've had some crazy thoughts."

"Like what?"

"I've got so much career energy pent up inside of me after all these years of caring for my kids, and now it's exploding, and I don't know what to do. I've been thinking of exploring journalism jobs in DC or New York and just coming home on the weekends."

"Wow! What does Ernie think?"

"I don't know. He just listens and nods with this perplexed look on his face. I'm not sure he knows who I am anymore. I'm not sure I do, either."

After winding up and down unfamiliar country roads, both of us grateful for Carol's GPS, we finally turn into a dirt driveway and head for a large barn.

"Where are we?" I ask as we walk up to the gathering crowd of mostly middle-aged women who have arrived for what I'm guessing is a workshop. A tall woman in a denim jacket says hello with an air of authority and points us in the direction of a row of metal chairs set up along the open side of the barn. That's when we catch our first glimpse of the star of the production. "A horse?"

"That's right," Carol says. "But this is no ordinary horse. She's going to inspire you. You'll see."

Tempted by the purr of the coffee maker they have out for the guests, I pour myself a cup, half wanting to let some of the hot java spill on my feet to thaw my toes. With fingers too numb to feel the Styrofoam cup, I pull a chair next to Carol, who has already taken her spot in a row of women.

I almost forget about the cold metal seat as I'm suddenly mesmerized by the uncanny interaction taking place between a man and his horse. As he moves about the ring with his horse, a foggy cloud of breath builds between the mare and her trainer. Morning frost still clings to the metal beams above, but the magic taking place in the ring is starting to warm me up. Carol shivers and coughs beside me. I lean closer and whisper, "Did you bring your asthma inhaler?"

"Don't worry. I'm fine," Carol says, but her cough tells me otherwise. Nonetheless, her eyes follow every move made by the man and the horse in front of us. It's as if they're dancing together, anticipating each other's every step. There's an almost visible connection between the two that requires no words, no signals, no prodding. They appear to be running on pure instinct and unwavering trust. Is this the message I'm supposed to get? Is this the inspiration? Maybe I *am* too much in my head these days and not in touch with my heart. I take a sideways glance at the row of women on the metal chairs next to me. Maybe I'm not the only one.

The trainer introduces himself and his lovely equine assistant. "I want to help you understand the power that's inside all of us to connect to ourselves and each other on a deep level," he says. As the horse follows the trainer's every move, his words seem to echo throughout the barn. *Connect to ourselves. Connect to each other. Connect on a deep level.*

As the trainer moves to the left, so does the mare. He takes three steps forward. She does the same. Their connection is undeniable. Unfortunately, so is the persistence of Carol's cough.

After an hour or so, there's a break in the workshop but not in the blustery air. Carol and I take refuge in her car, where she fires up the glorious, wonderful, amazing heat. That's when we two summer girls decide on taking a rain check on the rest of the program and promise to come back in the spring when it's warmer.

We head back to Jamestown for a brisk walk that leads us right past the most delicious buttery cinnamon air wafting from the bakery. We turn around and go in. As we make our way to the counter, a familiar voice calls to us. "Hey, Reets and Carol. Come sit with us."

It's Andrea, our friend from high school, the one who talked me into playing on the volleyball team and running at the beach for the first time. We pull up two chairs, then set down our coffee and muffins as Andrea introduces us to the five handsome young men at her table. They are all in their mid-twenties and in terrific shape. Andrea is amazingly relaxed and comfortable sitting there with them, one of the fringe benefits of her decision to join the town's volunteer fire department and rescue squad. That's what she's been up to since her youngest son left for college. "We just got off a rescue boat," she says, her merry brown eyes filled with pride. "We pulled a fisherman out of the ocean. Man was it cold!"

Although she doesn't know it, she's helping to rescue me, too. Sitting here in this bakery, sunlight streaming through the window, feeling the warmth of my two friends, I know I'm heading in the right direction with support and encouragement. I'm learning it's okay not to be in control, not to know where I'm going. I'm ready to let things unfold in the unexpected moment.

Sometimes you've got to quiet the cacophony in your head to take in all the inspiration that surrounds you. From a Saturday adventure you never expected. A walk that warms a chilly morning. A break in the bakery with your friends.

Even from a horse.

The Rocky Beach

In one of the cul-de-sacs in our neighborhood, there's a pathway that leads to the ocean. You'd have to know the path is there to find it, especially at this time of year after the growing season when the bushes are full and the grasses are high. It's been a while since I've meandered down this way, and I'm surprised once again by how steep and narrow the passage is, how the manicured lawn quickly gives way to dirt, scattered rocks, and gnarly tree roots heaving up from the ground, all demanding careful attention to my footing. Despite my cautiousness, the momentum of the slope takes hold and speeds up my gait. I pause for a moment to glance ahead at the bushes encroaching all around, a living green tunnel. Slowly, carefully, I keep heading down until I reach the shore. It's no easier here, though. I keep my eyes on the ground, trying to avoid the broken shells and slippery rocks scattered all around.

Another surprise awaits me. It's not the quiet morning I was anticipating, the calm oasis where I would gather my thoughts. The breeze blows in from the northwest, and waves lap up onto the shore. The tide has receded enough for me to walk, but it has left the rocks slick with seaweed. This has never been a beach for lounging on a towel. The narrow shoreline is like a strip of sandpaper, coarse and littered with stubble, shells, pebbles, and rocks.

Persisting to my destination, a giant boulder jutting out at the water's edge, I carefully climb to the top and settle into my thinking spot. My pondering perch. There, I take it all in. The gray-blue waters of Narragansett Bay. The dock on my right and the powerboat moored nearby, bobbing up and down in the choppy waves. In the distance, to my left, there's the outline of the Jamestown Bridge and the little mounds moving along its arches, cars transporting commuters to their jobs. But not me. I am here. My job is to think. My task is to untangle the mess in my mind and clear my vision so that when I make it back up the pathway and into my house, I will be in a better state than when I came.

So what happened when Meredith left for college? The gnawing emptiness. The incessant doubt. The persistent questions about who I am, what I should do, where I fit in. I'm like what would happen to that boat heaving around out there if, God forbid, a hurricane came our way and unleashed the tiny vessel from its berth, flinging it out into deep angry waters. I'm unmoored. Floating. Adrift. And I've got to figure it out.

It's loud out here. Wind whipping, water splashing, waves pounding on the rocks. Maybe I should get up and head back to where it's quiet. No. I'm going to stay. I've got to think.

Why does it work this way? One child, your youngest, moves 180 miles away, and in making that one change—that one transition that you had planned and expected and anticipated for years—you unleash many more. You start wondering about your marriage. How's that going to work now that you're alone with your husband?

And then your attention shifts to your parents, and you realize they need you more than ever before. It's been happening all along, of course, but you were too busy to do much about it. It's okay. It'll be okay. But it isn't. Now, with more time on your hands, you see what's going on with them in a new light.

If you're lucky, you've got your job to go to, the comfort of the day-to-day routine, your coworkers' familiar faces, and your favorite turkey and Swiss sandwich at the deli across the street. Or in my case, you stopped writing your newspaper column at the same time when your youngest left for college. Now what?

There's your house in a state of disrepair, demanding your attention. Your role with your kids is changing, easier at times and uncomfortable at others, fuzzy at best. You've got retirement decisions and money matters coming at you fast. Your friends take on new meaning. You start noticing they're going through changes, too. For the first time in a long while, the bits and pieces of the life you'd created for yourself don't fit together so well. You find yourself back at the drawing board.

To make it more challenging, you're not as present as you need to be. With all the free time and lack of structure, you're losing your bearings, your sense of time and place. One minute you're here, the next you're flashing back to times you thought you'd long forgotten: an embarrassing moment in the high school gym; a decisive night at an Italian restaurant with your husband; the first summer you needed a bra. It's as if the empty-nest crossroads has reshuffled the order of things in your gray matter, and you never know what's going to pop up.

Sitting here on this rock and taking stock of where I am reminds me of another time, decades ago, when I came here on a crystal-clear day in May stressed out from the pressures of running a business in Providence with my friend Joyce and our two new male partners. After hours of staring aimlessly at the sea and the sky, feeling the peace and the stillness, a wish came welling up inside of me. More than anything else, more than the business working out, more than success or fame and fortune, what I wished for so deeply was another child. A chance to make my family of three into four. A wish for Meredith.

We mothers have done it before. What begins as a wish, an inner knowing, we transform into a life. We nurture a family. We fashion a home. We come to this spot not knowing until we do know, and then we work with our hands and our hearts and make things happen. We make a place for ourselves and our families. We make home happen. We've done it before. We can do it again.

The Beethoven Breakfast

Stepping out of my car in the driveway of the house where I grew up, I'm greeted by the sound of a piano sonata drifting through the air. Beethoven, I think. Sonata Pathétique. I ring the doorbell knowing full well there's no chance my parents will hear it with the music up so loud, so I let myself in with my key. Still works. After all these years.

I find them seated at the kitchen table in the middle of their Sunday morning breakfast after church. "Hi Reets," says Dad as he gets up to pull out a chair for me and pour me a mug of coffee.

"Get yourself a plate," says Mom, offering me scrambled eggs, sizzling bacon, buttered toast, and fresh fruit. They are not just eating breakfast, mind you, they are dining. After six decades of marriage, they are making the most of this morning, enjoying a grand meal and each other's company with a little Beethoven thrown in for good measure. And these days, with more time on my hands and more questions on my mind, I can't think of a better place to look for answers.

Over the years, I've marveled, as have others, at my parents' ability to stay close. What's their secret? What magical formula do they possess that holds love together over the unexpected bumps and sharp turns, the slippery slopes and hidden valleys that inevitably rear their heads along the road, especially a road they've been traveling for so long?

"So, how do you do it?" I ask, settling into my seat and taking a sip of coffee. "Are you two so much alike that living together is easy, that breakfasts like this just happen because you get along so well and think alike after all this time?"

Mom smiles and looks over at my father. "Not exactly," says Dad. "You know how I am in the morning. I blast out of bed like a rocket, and that's before I've had my coffee. Your mom's not like that. She prefers to ease into her day." Maybe that's why he waits until she's washed and dressed before starting up a conversation. Maybe that's why she stays home and tends to daily chores while he runs errands each morning. Maybe differences can actually be good for a marriage when they're respected.

Several years ago, when my parents were painting their house, I noticed how well they worked together. She scraped, primed, and painted the windows. He took care of the shingles. Is it possible that teamwork is the secret to success?

"So, who's in charge when you're painting the house?" I ask Mom with a wink.

"It's simple," she says without missing a beat. "He's in charge of the red. I'm in charge of the white." In much the same way, he pays the bills, she washes the clothes. He mows the lawn. She dusts the furniture. The responsibility is shared, but the division of labor is clear. Red and white.

But how, I wondered, do two such very different people have fun together?

"It's easy," says Dad. "We make sure there's something in it for both of us. Like our recent trip to the factory outlets all over New England."

"You know I like to shop," says Mom. "And everyone knows how much Dad loves to drive. I came home with lots of good bargains, and your dad got to drive over six hundred miles!"

Mom gets up to clear our plates and brings the pot over to refill our coffee.

"How about when things don't go as planned?" I ask.

"Your mom always keeps her composure. She's sure and steady, and that helps me stay calm."

"And your dad is good at finding some humor in the situation. That helps us keep our perspective."

There's no denying it. When it comes to marriage, a sense of humor helps. As does the ability to stay calm, to compromise, to share responsibility, to work and play together, and to respect each other. But I've got a feeling there's something else. Nothing spectacular but important, nonetheless.

"Remember the time several elections ago when Mom was working at a nearby polling place? I love that story."

"Yes," she says with a smile. "I was putting in a long day, from six o'clock in the morning to nine o'clock at night. When I took a short break to drive to my home district to vote, your dad showed up to give me a ride." She shakes her head and laughs. "I told him I could have driven myself."

"And I told you," Dad says, reaching over for Mom's hand, "that then I wouldn't have gotten to see you all day."

And maybe that's the best secret of all. Maybe staying happily married is not so much about grand gestures as it is about the little things that light up an ordinary day. The simple things that don't need any elaborate planning, just a minute of thoughtfulness. The Sunday breakfast with Beethoven. The one going out of their way for the other. Appreciating each other. Not wanting to miss a day or an hour or a moment together. Wishing that time like this could just go on and on and on.

I wish so, too. I hope. I pray.

Kicking It

The navy-blue sweater I bought last weekend reminded me of the summer I wore the same cardigan every day. I think I was ten at the time, maybe eleven. No matter how hot or humid or downright sweltering the day, that sweater became part of my summer uniform—shorts, tank top and navy-blue security garment. There I was in the field behind our house on one of those rare occasions when the neighborhood boys needed someone else—even a girl!—to play kickball. I'd be out there trying to prove myself, running the bases and catching fly balls with that wool sweater clinging to my back, beads of sweat dripping from my armpits. What I should have done was ask Mom if we could go bra shopping. I was too uncomfortable to do that. I suspected she might have felt the same.

This was one of the many things we hesitated talking about. Our eventual discussion about "the birds and the bees" consisted of an awkward handing off of a little green book that Mom said I should keep in the drawer of my bedside table. I don't recall actually reading it, just peeking at the squiggly line drawings of the inner workings of the female body. "If you have questions, let me know," I remember her saying. I also remember thinking that I would never do that. I would never ask anyone anything about any of that. Eventually, however, I did. What are girlfriends for?

In my mind, the navy-blue sweater was a perfectly rational solution.

After all, I had grown accustomed to uniforms. Every morning before grade school, I had pulled on the plaid jumper, white blouse, and red knee socks that were required at St. Lucy's School where the nuns took on the challenge of teaching a curious and rambunctious group of children how to become good Catholic boys and girls. In seventh grade, we girls would trade in our jumpers for plaid skirts and gray vests. I think we all knew the wardrobe change had less to do with distinguishing us as upperclassmen than it did with the straps of our jumpers beginning to protrude in provocative ways that called attention to what was blossoming underneath. The gray vests did a better job of covering all that up.

Just like the navy-blue sweater. It had been hard enough trying to convince the neighborhood boys who were always having so much fun playing kickball to give me a chance. But wearing that thing made it even harder.

"How ya gonna play with that sweater on?" they'd holler before breaking into uncontrollable laughter. "What are you trying to hide?"

The boys were never too keen on the idea of me joining in, but once in a while, if they were short players and needed some amusement, they'd let me on the field. To be honest, I wasn't very fast running the bases, or quick enough to catch every outfield fly, but I sure could kick that ball. Even so, I wasn't always welcome. Kickball was a boys' game on the boys' field. As Dad said to Mom in a voice loud enough for me to overhear "Rita shouldn't be out there with the boys."

There were a lot of *shouldn'ts* in those days. We shouldn't miss Mass on Sundays, and we shouldn't eat meat on Fridays. We shouldn't question our parents, and we shouldn't speak to adults unless we were spoken to. We shouldn't wear dresses or skirts when all the other girls were wearing cable knit sweaters and Levis, and our hair had to be long and straight even if that meant positioning our heads awkwardly on ironing boards every morning to steam out all the natural curls and waves. We grew up learning the virtues of conformity and uniformity, sitting in rows and standing in lines, playing by the rules and fitting into the roles.

Until suddenly it all blew up.

The first tremor I recall shook our bus on the way home from school one dark November day. The boys were talking about the news from Dallas, an urgent bulletin that couldn't possibly have been true. But when I got home and gathered with my family around the TV in the living room, the images were undeniable: our young president slumped over in the backseat of the open limousine; Jackie in her pink suit dappled with blood, cradling her fallen husband; and the Secret Service men at the back of the car as it sped through the crowd.

Change was an earthquake that began to shake us from every direction, shattering rules and mores, ways of living and thinking and being. It was as if the adolescent tumult inside of me was reflected in the chaos all around. There were more assassinations, along with a war on poverty that was overshadowed by the war in Vietnam. The Vatican decreed that the Latin Mass we never understood could be said in English, and by the way, women no longer needed to cover their heads before entering church. Birth control became available as a convenient pill. The cigarettes our parents had smoked for as long as we could remember were deemed hazardous to our health. We sent a man to the moon. Everywhere we looked, boundaries were crossed, and norms were upended. All the years of quiet conformity erupted into protests on campuses and buses, in front of the United Nations, and on the National Mall in Washington, DC, on a bridge in Alabama, and at a bar in Greenwich Village. On the boardwalk outside the Miss America pageant in Atlantic City, women stood protesting among the crowd, burning the very undergarments I had reluctantly asked my mother to buy.

Viewing the Miss America pageant in this new light stoked an anger inside of me white, hot, and seething. As a young chubby girl, I had grown up watching the televised spectacle every year, idolizing a feminine ideal that seemed aspirational yet unattainable. The 36–24–36. The long legs strutting up and down the catwalk in bathing suits and high heels. No wonder the boys that lined the walls of our English hall in high school had gotten the idea that rating female students was okay, that they could whistle, bark, hoot, and howl as we girls walked by. So what if a particularly nasty jeer rang in our ears for the rest of the day or longer? They were just boys being boys on their way to men being men.

We were on the brink of seismic change, and I saw an opening. My life could be vastly different from my mother's; my choices could reach beyond who I might marry, how many kids I'd bring into the world, and what kind of home I'd make for my family. My girlfriends and I would embrace a burgeoning world of almost limitless possibilities for women, facing most of them without role models. And yet, along with the blessing of all that potential would come the curse of how we were actually going to manage it all.

Clearly, the guardrails I'd clung to when I was growing up were disappearing, and I'd have to find my own footing, something I'd have to do again and again and again. It would be years, decades in fact, before I would figure it out. You could say that here in this empty-nest chapter of my life, I still am. And you would be right.

But in the years immediately following the cardigan summer, with doors opening and closing all around, I began to realize a few things about my life for certain: I was going to get out there on the boys' field and kick that ball, and I wouldn't need the navy-blue sweater after all.

It's Just How He Rolls

The first time it happens, Meredith has only been away at college for a month or two.

It's one of those perfect fall days, sunny but not quite hot enough for the beach. Ernie and I are heading there for a long barefoot walk along the shoreline, anticipating that we'll have the warm sand and glistening waves pretty much to ourselves since most of the tourists have gone home. As we drive along, we chat about the meeting he had the other day, the book I'm reading, and whether we'll stop for ice cream later.

And then, just like that, the conversation comes to a halt. His head swivels toward the open window, his eyes riveted on some passing distraction. Despite the attentive wife beside him, he lets out a long, low whistle.

I scan the sidewalk for the object of his attention. Is she blond? A redhead perhaps? But all I see are two men in business suits talking on their cell phones.

"Sweet," Ernie says.

That's when I catch a glimpse of her. It's hard not to notice how he looks at her with longing. The bold curve of her shoulders, the subtle tilt of her rear end. Her long nose, in elegant contrast to her sinewy body. She is classy. She is polished. She is . . . a roadster.

Truth be told, these stolen glances are nothing new in our

marriage. How the shiny flash of chrome and steel lures his attention away. How the purr of an engine causes him to freeze mid-sentence and forget everything.

Except for her. The fast one coming up behind him with her top down.

All these years later, you'd think I'd have become accustomed to my husband's love affair with cars. When I was busier, I never gave it more than a passing thought. But here in the courtship of our newfound freedom, I find myself holding each piece up to the light, considering this, reconsidering that. It's as if I'm constructing the puzzle for the first time.

Maybe I'm not the only one.

Not long after our trip to the beach, we're wandering along Bowen's Wharf in Newport on a sunny Saturday with no particular destination in mind when Ernie abruptly stops in his tracks. He turns and faces me.

"I've got a question," he says.

"Sure," I say, hesitating right there in front of the sunglasses shop.

"If you were going to buy a Jeep CJ-5 and it were only available in two colors, say bright yellow or dark green, which would you pick?"

I start to laugh, but the look on his face tells me my husband expects an answer. Right here. Right now. Doesn't matter that we're not in the market for a car. Doesn't matter that I have no idea what a Jeep CJ-5 looks like. Just answer the question. Let me see. I like green. I like yellow. Don't think. Just pick.

"Yellow," I say, focusing my gaze on the boats in the nearby harbor.

"Great! So far, so good," he says. "Mercedes 500. Midnight blue or red?"

"Blue."

"That's the right answer!" Ernie is smiling like a teacher who just saw a light bulb going off in his student's head.

"It is?"

"We're definitely on the same wavelength."

"We are?"

Now that I've passed some sort of marital compatibility quiz, the kind they must publish in *Motor Trend* or *Car and Driver*, I'd like to tell you we walked off happily into our new life together, rediscovering each other at every turn. The rediscovery part is true. But as fun and exhilarating as rediscovering each other can be at times, there are other moments. Perhaps you know the ones. Perhaps you've felt the fear and the doubt rise in your belly, and suddenly you're uncomfortable. You start questioning things. Things you'd rather not think about. Especially now, with more time on your hands.

But I'm also finding that having more time can be good. And spending some of it in his world and on his interests can be illuminating. And sometimes, quite hilarious.

Like a few months later when we're shopping for a new car. I'm standing in the showroom, sandwiched between Ernie and a salesman. Somehow, color doesn't seem at the top of anyone's list.

"Four-wheel drive?" asks my husband.

"Of course," replies the dealer, smoothing a wrinkle in his jacket.

Ernie's eyes light up. "How's the compression ratio?"

"Excellent. Coefficient of drag is decent. Torque's right up there, too."

"Great!" Ernie leans in closer. "McPherson struts?"

"Definitely. And check this out," the dealer says, pointing to a photo in a brochure on his desk. "GPS nav system. Accurate to 1.3 meters, give or take a centimeter."

"Wheels?"

"Low-profile eighteen-inch alloy rims with five spokes."

"What do you think?" Ernie turns to me, searching my face for approval. The salesman waits anxiously for my reply.

I want to say something like *I want a car that starts up when you turn the key. I want a car that's good for hauling groceries and suitcases. I want a car I can drive without a degree in mechanical engineering.*

I want to. But the words won't come. So I just smile a low-profile-kind-of-wife smile and say to my husband the only thing I can think of: "It all depends on if you know the answer to my question."

"What's your question?"

"Moonlight silver or jet black?"

She's Back! And I Am, Too.

Ernie and I don't know what to expect as we head to New York City on a perfect fall Friday to pick up our freshman. With so much stuff to pack into the car for her long weekend home, you'd think Meredith wasn't planning on going back to school anytime soon.

Settling into the backseat, her eyes light up as she fills us in on the details. In a few short weeks, she has managed to live on her own in one of the most difficult cities in the world, make some new friends, find her way to classes, and, for the most part, keep up with the work. The excitement in her voice carries us the 180 miles home in a flash. How wonderful to see our daughter come home in such a jubilant mood.

Saturday's warm sunshine inspires us to take a leisurely walk with Lizzie, rustling through leaves past neighbors' houses where Meredith used to babysit, where she once played with her friends as a child. "Last summer, I could never have imagined hanging out in Washington Square Park with my roommate, or taking the subway to the film bookstore on the West Side," she says, smiling with an almost visible sense of pride.

Later, we celebrate her homecoming with dinner at her favorite restaurant and a visit to our favorite ice cream stand; everything is so familiar, which makes the change in her all the more striking. How much she's grown in just a matter of weeks!

Sunday brings more good times together. For walking and talking. For taking a trip over the bridge to get coffee and tea and driving around, allowing her to reacquaint herself with the shingle-style cottages and the ocean views, the impossibly green lawns dissected by rambling stone walls and pink rose gardens. A welcome reprieve, I suspect, from the towering buildings and the bustling sidewalks. Back at home, she tackles her homework while we parents kick back and watch football. So relaxing. And I had worried about the transition, how we'd all fit back together again.

The Monday holiday arrives, and the pace quickens. We're hosting a dinner party to celebrate Geoff's birthday. He's driving down from Boston, and we're being joined by my dad and mom, my sister Denise, and her husband, Claude. I shift into high gear, shopping, cleaning, cooking, and setting up. We've been hosting these family birthday celebrations for many years, and just as with any ritual, there's a familiar comfort to the gathering. Denise and Claude bring a large salad, and Geoff stops at the bakery for a couple loaves of bread. Dad pours the water, and Mom helps me serve. We all take our seats at the table, except for Lizzie, who paces up, down, and all around in the hope that a crouton, a carrot, or a bit of salmon will slip off a fork and come her way.

"How's the new job going in Boston?" Dad asks the birthday boy—I mean, young man. And then Dad turns to his granddaughter. "How do you like living in New York?"

New job in Boston. Living in New York. How is it that we can gather the same faces in the same places and yet nothing is the same? There will be one more candle on Geoff's cake this year. As I set the bowl of roasted potatoes down and sink into my chair at the end of the table, across from Ernie, I suddenly feel tired. And we haven't even begun eating. Let alone cleaning up.

Not that it's a good time to be tired. Tuesday is the leaving day when Meredith packs her things and heads back to school. We've got a lot to do.

Before heading south to New York City, we make an early morning trip north to the mall in Providence, just mother and daughter, to get her cell phone repaired. With a little time to spare, we find a pair of jeans in our favorite department store, a gift from me before she goes back. Before *we* go back.

"Do you want to look at boots?" I ask, taking a few strides toward the shoe department. "We've got about a half hour."

"Not really."

"How about grabbing coffee and tea for the ride back?"

"I'm all set."

"You sure?"

Abruptly, she stops walking and stares down at the shiny floor. I stand there awkwardly, waiting for her to catch her breath, regain her composure.

"I think I ate too much this weekend," she says. Before I can assure her that we all did and she'll get right back on track, she adds on. "I've got too much work to do. I don't know how I'm ever going to get it all done."

"You will. You're off to such a good start."

"It doesn't feel like it. It's too much. I just don't think I can do this, Mom."

I glance over at the mannequin standing near us, the one with the leopard skin coat and the smug look on her face. Maybe she'd know what to say.

"I just can't," Meredith says, standing in the middle of the store in the middle of the mall. "I can't go back."

As we slowly make our way to the parking garage, I struggle to reconcile the jubilant daughter we picked up on Friday with the one who is here with me now, just a few short and seemingly pleasant days later. The triumphant return seems to be fading into a dim memory. The conqueror of the city is retreating into the familiar scenery of the countryside right before my eyes.

Back at home, I pack the car while she takes a shower. Geoff helps, all the while talking about a problem he's dealing with at work. The details are a bit technical, something about social media and a product promotion he's planning. I'm packing. I'm listening. I'm piecing together most of what he's saying. But despite my best intentions to stay in the present moment, I find myself marveling at the irony here. Our kids still need us! Of course, they do. Somehow, during all my introspection and struggle during the last month or so, I hadn't been thinking that our role as parents would keep on going much the same as ever. Only different.

After more delays and an extra-long goodbye to Lizzie, who slouches in the corner of the entryway, her nose down on the wooden floor, Meredith is ready to go. The ride back to New York is longer than usual.

"It's hard to make the transition," I say, looking at our daughter slumped over in the backseat and staring out the window. "You'll be back into your classes and your routine, and you'll feel better."

"Thanksgiving is almost here," I say. "You'll soon be heading back home, bringing your new friend Chase along with you for the extra-long weekend, and you can relax for a while."

She sighs deeply and looks down at her shoes. Our talkative girl is silent. The car rolls on. Time does the same.

On the long drive home, Ernie and I stop at a rest area and buy two bottles of iced tea and an oversized bag of pretzels.

"It'll be good to get back to our new normal," he says as we get back onto the road.

"I guess."

"What's wrong?"

"I feel so mixed up."

"How so?"

"For a few short days this weekend, everything felt so right. I knew what I was doing. I knew what was expected of me. Now I've got to go back and face 'the new normal,' as you call it."

"You'll get used to it."

In a strange way, I'm looking forward to it. Which makes me happy. And sad. All at the same time.

Here's what they neglect to mention in the books and articles about what to expect when your youngest child goes off to college: she'll come back. And the independent life she's beginning to create for herself, just like the one you're trying to create for yourself, is tenuous at best, not yet sturdy enough to withstand all the familiar cues and ingrained patterns of returning home.

Shifting gears is easy for a car. But we're not cars. Transitions take time. Transitions laced with emotions take longer. The families we raised, the homes we created, these were built upon countless moments in which we gave what we had. And even more than that. We helped with algebra homework. We stayed up all night to nurse a child with a fever. We showed up for soccer games, tennis matches, and ballet recitals. Gradually, we became inextricably entwined in the fabric of our family as our days turned into months into years. So why wouldn't we expect that it would take us some time and tender care to loosen the strings of all we've woven so tightly together?

The Merlot Decision

On a chilly October evening, Ernie surprises me with dinner reservations at a little Italian restaurant in the nearby town of Narragansett. We open the door and walk into a charming place aglow in flickering candlelight.

"Good evening," says the waiter as he escorts us to a small table in the back of the room and pulls out a chair for me.

"This is perfect," I say to Ernie. "We haven't been here in a long time. What a nice idea!"

In a short while, the waiter returns. I order a glass of chardonnay. Ernie asks for a merlot. And that's when it hits me. The last time we were here, we had a life-changing conversation. Ah, yes, The Merlot Decision. I remember.

How many years have passed since that evening, I couldn't tell you. But what I do recall is Ernie sitting across a small table just like this one, tilting his glass, his dark eyes following the merlot, floating back and forth as if in a trance. The subject at hand was nothing new. In our marriage, it seemed that all turning points—a new house, a new job, a new school—inevitably led to the same question. Two careers plus two children equals what kind of family? How do you do what's right for the individuals as well as the group?

At the time, Ernie had just accepted a position at an advertising agency in Boston that would require a ninety-minute commute on good traffic days and long hours away from home in exchange for a salary that would more than cover our needs. This happened to coincide with the week that Geoff stayed home from school not due to injury or illness but rather because his parents thought it was a school vacation. It was not. Despite all our late nights, the equitable division of household tasks, and hiring a part-time nanny, our family life never seemed to settle into a comfortable rhythm. Ernie's new job and commute would only add to the chaos. Something had to give.

He took another sip of wine and wished for a simpler time. A life free of the frustrations and pressures that can weigh so heavily on a man, a husband, a father.

Attempting to ease his mind, I mentioned, in a passing kind of way, that I could always go back to working full-time. After all, I'd spent my share of time climbing the corporate ladder. I still knew the ropes, and I knew them well.

For the first time that night, I detected a shy smile curling up at the corners of his mouth. Perhaps it was because of the wine, or the warm glow from the candle, but he was about to reveal a bit of his soul that I'd never seen before. It was something I could have easily guessed, I suppose, but hearing it from his lips would profoundly change the way I looked at things from that moment on.

"Maybe it's chivalry," he had said. "Maybe I'm old-fashioned, but I just don't want you to have to do what I do."

In days gone by, such a comment would have grated against my sense of equality, and I would have girded for battle. In a heartbeat, I would have convinced myself that it was a plot, a maneuver as devious as it was shrewd. In my mind, he would head for the bright lights of fame and fortune, leaving me, quite literally, in the dust.

But it had been a long and winding road that led me to that

table where I sat across from him. Face-to-face. Eye-to-eye. Man-to-woman. And at that point in my travels, it had felt wonderful to have someone who wanted to protect me. Someone who wanted to look out for me and our children. I had clawed my way there as a single mother. I had achieved success with my marketing consulting business. And I had stood for more than a few moments staring out the window of my second-floor office watching our nanny play with Meredith out on the lawn, wondering when she was going to grow out of wanting to play out on the lawn and pondering if I would still be watching out the window when that happened.

Ever since that night of the Merlot Decision, I had managed to shift gears from the hard-driving, ambitious career professional to fully embrace my mission of motherhood. It wasn't easy at first. I drove by the post office at least a dozen times with the letters of resignation I had written to my clients sitting on the dashboard before actually dropping them in the box. But change, as tough as it was, ushered in a happier time for us and an unexpected new career opportunity for me. I began writing about family life as a way to preserve the fleeting moments. Eventually, I was lucky enough to share my observations in a weekly *Providence Journal* column, a career move I could never have envisioned, one that fit me like none that had come before.

Maybe this empty-nest change we're going through will bring new opportunities for us again.

"Hey, honey! You seem so far away," says Ernie as our waiter returns to take our order.

"No. I'm here."

Ernie takes my hand in his.

"I was just remembering another night. Another glass of merlot."

"Like this one," Ernie says as he squeezes my hand.

In that moment, I realize that as hard and uncomfortable as transitions can be, they can also usher in something entirely fresh and magical, something we can't even imagine. As long as we stay open to the possibilities.

Oh, Canada!

He's gone.

Just like that, my father packed up his car and left for Montreal to visit his brother.

In the past, Dad's travels would have been no big deal. I would have called to wish him a good time, a safe trip. A week or so later, when he returned, I would have asked how it went, listened to the details of his adventure, and caught up on all the news of my uncle.

But everything has changed. Mom is no longer willing—or possibly able—to accompany Dad to Canada. She's putting her foot down. After all the road trips she made as a young navy wife, crisscrossing the country from Washington, DC, to San Diego, to Newport, Rhode Island, and back to California again, followed by settling in Newport only to retire there and drive to California every winter, she is finally saying no. She won't go. And no one, not even her dear husband, can convince her otherwise.

So Dad is going alone. Even though he's in his eighties, he's a good driver, and I'm not worried about him. My mom, well, that's a different story.

The trip to Canada has required my sister and me to rearrange our schedules, to cobble together a patchwork of care for Mom. I'll take the days since I've got more free time now. Denise will take the nights to accommodate her work schedule. We sisters will meter out our time and move back into the house where we grew up to give Mom a hand, to give Dad a break. We'll be there to smooth out the edges and do whatever is needed until Dad returns.

The challenges with Mom have been mounting slowly but surely. I think Denise was the first to notice. Dad picked up on it, too. I preferred to look the other way, fabricating perfectly logical reasons for Mom slowing down, not remembering where she left her glasses, or forgetting that I told her I would stop by. So much is going on, I thought. So what if something slipped her mind? It's just one little thing. And then another. But nothing big. Nothing of consequence. It happens to all of us. In my mind, at least, there are plenty of logical reasons to explain her behavior. Extremely logical. Except for one problem. They have nothing to do with the truth.

I don't like the truth.

Dad insists on saying things I don't want to hear: "Mom seems to be losing ground lately. She needs more help every day." He tells me he's driving, shopping, cooking, and cleaning. He's washing, bathing, feeding, and caring. He's compensating, coping, hoping, and praying. And praying some more.

Denise keeps pointing to the symptoms I've read about on websites and learned in the Alzheimer's course I took to reassure myself that none of this was really happening to our mother. She says, "Mom loses her thought in the middle of a sentence. She forgets what she heard just moments before. She searches for words that won't come, making sounds that trail off in the distance." A distance that's growing way too quickly.

It's hard even for me to deny the connections Mom is severing one by one. The friends she refuses to see any longer. Her sister who calls from across the country only to find no answer on this end of the line. The circle of comfort and support that grows smaller and smaller, the world closing in on Mom while we stand by helplessly, watching her fade into a shadow of her once-sunny self.

As surely as Alzheimer's affects my mother's brain, fear grips mine. Denial—not hearing, not seeing, not listening, not comprehending— these are my inadequate defenses. Let's get to the truth about fear. Defenses will not work. The only way out is through. Face the truth. Name it. See it. Feel it. Embrace it in all its majestic awfulness.

With every day that passes, the fear I've been avoiding grows in the back of my mind. Every time I see my mother, it lurks and prowls, no matter how hard I try making it disappear. Will this be the day she pushes *me* away, too? Not intentionally, of course. But what if I reach out to hug her and she looks at me with the puzzled expression that has replaced her gracious countenance so much of the time? What if she searches my face, my eyes for some recognition, some recollection, and, just like that, the connection is lost? What once was there, the closeness, the unconditional love and support, will be ripped away by this unforgiving stranger, this uninvited guest. The flame will flicker and go out. She won't know me.

She. Won't. Know. Me.

But I'm here with her now while Dad is away, and thank God, she knows who I am. So why go down that dark path when a more pleasant one is right in front of us?

"Come on, Mom. Let's go on an adventure."

She looks up at me, hesitating for a moment, and then smiles. I help her with her jacket and get her settled into the front seat of my car.

"Where?" she asks.

"I can't tell you. It's a surprise."

She claps her hands and leans forward in her seat, looking at the road ahead of us. Out of the corner of my eye, I see her smiling.

The ride is short and very sweet, with the flaming leaves of autumn painting a fall portrait outside the windows. What a perfect way to set the mood for our destination.

Before long, we arrive at an orchard in the nearby countryside where we can pick our own apples. The crisp, clean air greets us as we stroll over to the stand and ask for a few bags. Before I can decide which way to go, Mom heads down a path amid rows of fruit-laden trees, one bag in each hand. "Look at all the apples!" She points to McIntosh, Macoun, and Cortland and starts filling her bags.

Maybe this place brings back memories of her growing up on a farm in Minnesota, a happy return to nature found in the simple joy of picking food from a tree. There's no way to know what's happening inside of her. But the pep in her step and the determination in her eyes as she goes from tree to tree picking as many apples as our bags will hold tells me all I need to know about this day, this time spent with her.

Soon we are driving over the Newport Bridge. "Look! All the boats!" she says, enjoying the spectacular view of the harbor.

When we arrive at my house, I help her up the front steps and usher her into a cozy seat in the family room. She's greeted by her wet-nosed friend, Lizzie, who plops down at Mom's feet, a warm hug on a chilly day.

From my spot in the kitchen where I'm chopping our apples and mixing them together with flour, sugar, and spice, I see my mom sitting there, her head beginning to nod as she drifts off into a nap. After a while, she awakens to the smell of cinnamon, followed by a steaming cup of tea, and a warm slice of apple bread straight from the oven.

I sit next to her on the couch. I close my eyes for a moment, breathing it all in: the cinnamon, the apples, the warmth and comfort of the family room. Just Mom and me watching Lizzie sniff around for crumbs. Content together here in the autumn afternoon.

The Pink Flower and the Yellow Balls

"**D**id you leave this flower here for me?" I remember saying that all those years ago to my new friend on the other side of the cubicle wall at the advertising agency where we had both recently been hired. The pink blossom had surprised me, set there in a vase among the papers, the mail, the files, my coffee mug, my pencils, and my planner—Sharon's lovely acknowledgment of the secret we shared.

We had quickly bonded, two fresh-faced, educated women ready to take on the world, which, we were learning, still very much belonged to our male colleagues. Unlike in college, we would no longer succeed or fail based upon hard work and aptitude. Success, we realized, was going to require toughness and some new competitive strategies.

Maybe that's why I kept my secret for as long as I did, until my growing belly and flowing dresses began giving me away. One of the agency's owners clarified management's position when I assured them I'd return to work after my maternity leave. "Three women who worked for us in the past told us they'd come back, too. None of them actually did. Of course, we hope you'll be different."

I *was* different. After Geoff was born, I did come back to the desk in the cubicle alongside Sharon. A year later, she left to move with her new husband to begin his medical practice in Arizona, and I moved to another position at another agency. Years flew by with just a Christmas card or two between us until she ended up back in Rhode Island with a provocative idea for how we could stay in touch.

"You've got to be kidding!" That's what I said when she first proposed her plan. "An hour? For tennis?" As much as I loved the game, I had given up all but an occasional match since starting a family and a business. With all the demands on my time, how could I spare sixty minutes a week just for fun?

How could I not?

As I quickly discovered, fun comes at you fast. Every Friday morning, Sharon and I met at the indoor courts and smashed that yellow ball back and forth, harder and faster, driving and striving for every point with the kind of intensity you'd expect from two finalists at Wimbledon. We kept serving and volleying, lobbing and rushing, hitting and running until we were sweating and breathless. And then we'd do it some more.

Sharon was taller than me, and her shoulders and arms were strong from years of swimming. My best chance of winning seemed to lie in my legs. I had to run all over the court for every ball. Almost every ball.

"You two are becoming fanatics!" said the players on the court next to us. They couldn't help noticing that we kept playing when our hour was up. Just one more point. Again and again and again. Until the next group finally assembled and set claim to their rightful territory.

That's when Sharon and I retreated to the locker room, not for the shower or even to change our clothes but rather to sink into the chairs there. While our heart rates settled into a more normal rhythm, we'd invariably find ourselves caught up in conversation. We could talk about anything from our day-to-day challenges to our lifelong dreams. There were no rules. No boundaries. Just a flow of innermost thoughts. Unedited sound bites from the lives of two wives. Two mothers. Two dreamers. Two friends.

"You two still talking?" asked one of the players from the other court, poking her head into the locker room. "After watching you trying to kill each other on the court, it's nice to see you getting along."

When summer breezed in, and our indoor court time expired, it got harder to play each week. Harder to justify. The kids were out of school. Schedules were looser. Vacations were planned. And still, we managed to play.

One of my favorite times was Sunday, seven o'clock in the morning. How could anyone like the hour when the only human sighted during my ten-mile trek to the courts was the toll collector on the Newport Bridge? But that, of course, was the point. Once I pried myself out of bed, I'd see how wonderful the world was when it was just waking up.

There's nothing quite like arriving at the courts of a nearby boarding school set high atop a hill overlooking the Atlantic Ocean in the early morning quiet of a perfect summer's day. Since Sharon lived closer, she'd usually beat me there, waiting for me with a smile and two cups of coffee. Being the only two zealots there at that hour, our chatter would fill the air like the chirping of mourning doves.

But this past year, something changed. You'd think that with Meredith off in New York, I'd have more time to play. And some days, it seemed like all I had was time, way too much of it. Maybe the pressure of juggling too many things for too long had caught up with me. Maybe the stress of all the decisions I felt I needed to make about my career, the house, and our lives going forward was taking a toll. I'm not sure exactly what, but something compelled me to clear my schedule, to deconstruct everything before creating something new.

So when it came time to commit to another year of indoor tennis, I wavered.

"What if we don't play? When will I ever see you?" Sharon asked.

"That's silly," I was quick to respond.

But she made me think. It was no different with my other friends, how difficult it was sometimes to schedule a lunch, or a Girls' Night, or even a walk. And I knew Sharon was right. Yet I persisted in giving myself a blank canvas. Some white space. An empty court without a racket or a yellow ball.

Maybe sometimes we need to slow down. Take a break. Free our schedules. Maybe our heads get twisted up in a muddle, and our intentions become murky because we're always going, doing, pushing, pursuing, and competing.

What if we stopped long enough to create a space in time for ourselves to think and ponder and be still?

What if we gave ourselves permission to just be? Not forever. Just long enough to see what happens.

See what's in there. See what could be revealed if we dare to slow down and listen.

Sweet Indulgence

Ten years or so ago, on a weekend getaway to Martha's Vineyard with Ernie, I came across a cookbook on a shelf at our favorite café, Espresso Love. Its recipes revealed the owners' secrets, the ones that have kept their customers coming back day after day or, in our case, year after year. Holding the book in my hands and fanning through pages of spectacular island photos, I got a glimpse of the life I envisioned for my husband and me when and if things ever calmed down. Family and friends gathered around a table set with healthy and delicious food. Long, leisurely walks at the seashore collecting shells, searching for hidden treasure. A life that allowed time for browsing the local farmers market for fresh ingredients, pondering new recipes, and baking instead of settling for a powdered mix in a package from the bakery. There, relaxed and renewed on vacation with that cookbook in my hands, I could almost see it. I could almost taste it.

And then, just like that, the boom came crashing to the ground. *It's not going to happen,* I told myself. Not anytime soon. Maybe never. Not with two kids, a dog, a column to write, and a business to run, all waiting for me when I return to the mainland.

I put the book back on the shelf, walked away, and boarded the ferry back to reality.

As it turned out, I wasn't the only one who liked the ideas in those pages. Ernie wanted to hold on to that vision of a calmer life, and so he thoughtfully bought the cookbook as a surprise. "Someday, we'll get there," he said. Never mind that someday was a distant ship on the horizon, barely visible to our bleary eyes.

But now, amazingly, someday is here!

It's here in the kitchen, where I stand at the counter with Lizzie eagerly watching my every move, following me from one cabinet to the next, from the mixer to the bowl to the oven, with her tail wagging every step of the way. I've got my Martha's Vineyard cookbook perched on a stand in the middle of the counter, the colorful pages fanned open to my favorite section. That would be desserts.

I love everything about making them. The lemon squares and the cocoa bars. The raspberry turnovers and the overstuffed apple pie. I love the way I can take all the disparate ingredients that by themselves are nothing much: tasteless white flour; sour lemons; salty baking powder; unsweetened, almost bitter cocoa. But then I stir them all up in a bowl and, magically, they blend into something so much more than anything I could have imagined.

There's enjoyment in this long-awaited luxury of time. Unrushed. Unhurried. Lost in my baking meditation, the only reminder of reality is the kitchen timer. I appreciate that the gratification of what I'm doing is anything but instant, that I have to wait for the warm oven to do its work, that 350 degrees will eventually transform milky batter into sweet indulgence.

I breathe in the aroma that fills the house, a delicious hint of what's to come. But there's more to all this than the irresistible smell would lead you to believe.

Desserts, at least in our house, are reserved for accompanying a special meal. They're a treat brought along to a party or baked to serve guests on a holiday or some other festive celebration. A German chocolate cake for a birthday. A strawberry tart for a dinner party with friends. Treats like these are a departure from the routine, a little splurge in calories. Butter. Sugar. Chocolate. All the decadent things we don't tend to eat on a regular basis. Dessert is sweet permission to break away from the mundane, to sit back and savor the moment, to take back something that the hectic days might threaten to steal away.

This particular baking day, with the cold November rain pelting hard on the rooftop, is delicious to me in so many ways. With a house full of company heading our way for Thanksgiving, I'm setting aside the entire afternoon just for creating desserts.

The entire afternoon just for creating desserts!

There are empty-nest moments like this that show up as pleasant surprises if we give ourselves permission to enjoy them. Slowing down to savor the anticipation of the holiday. Losing ourselves in the hours of sweet preparation. All of which would have been unthinkable in the years that came before, undoable in all the overscheduled days, especially with Thanksgiving quickly approaching. We'd have been lucky to make it to the grocery store to fetch the turkey and all its fixings without having to squeeze in a few phone calls in the parking lot or tend to one kid or errand or crisis along the way.

But that was then.

Here I am alone in my quiet kitchen. Just me and my enthusiastic canine assistant. And in the next three or four hours, my only mission is to mix, beat, and stir together enough alchemy to result in one pumpkin pie, one chocolate cheesecake, and one ginger spice cake with lemon icing, hopefully all coming out of the oven as delicious as they look in the photographs from my island cookbook. The one that captured my eye and illustrated my hope for the future all those years ago.

The New Parents

In the moonlight, wearing my heels and pink dress, I step carefully across the parking lot. "What a lovely wedding," I say to Ernie, who holds the car door open for me. "So nice to see my cousins again."

"They sure put on a first-class event," Ernie says, settling into the driver's seat. "And it was great seeing your mom and dad on the dance floor. They stole the show!"

They sure did! Even though Mom is slowing down these days, you'd never know it when Dad's got her in his arms.

A knock on the window startles me. My sister waits, shivering in her dress on this chilly evening. I open the window.

"I was thinking, Reets. Now that Meredith is in college, maybe you could spend a few days a week at Mom and Dad's. It would be great for Dad to have help, and some time to get out and do errands, or go see his friends."

"*Hmmm.* I'll think about it."

"Okay. Let me know."

"Have a good ride home." I close the window and stare out into the night, watching Denise and Claude walk to their car.

"Maybe I could spend a few days a week at Mom and Dad's?" I shake my head.

"Bad timing," Ernie says. "We were having such a fun evening."

Denise isn't wrong. Mom definitely needs more help these days.

Dad could use more support. It's just that Ernie and I have finally reached a point on our parenting journey where our youngest is away at college and our lives seem to be getting a little more carefree.

A week or so goes by, and then Denise suggests going for a walk. "Sure," I say. Over the years, walking with my sister has become one of my favorite things. Sometimes, we walk more than we talk. Other times, we talk more than we walk.

As I've come to appreciate, there's no one better to talk with than my sister. As soon as I see her, my filters are instinctively off, my shields down. Anything I say is okay with her. Good. Bad. Smart. Stupid. No need to weigh my thoughts or measure my words. She knows what I mean. Even when I don't.

As we stroll down the sidewalk in East Greenwich, a town that's roughly halfway between our homes, I wonder what we'll talk about today. Her job? My writing? Her house renovation? My kids? A poetry book she's reading? A movie we just have to go see?

"We've got to come up with a plan." There's a look in her eye, a determination in the way she sets her chin that lets me know she means business.

"What sort of plan?"

"For Mom and Dad. Things are changing quickly with Mom. Dad needs more help. I thought we could brainstorm some ways that we can be there for them." She picks up the pace.

"Okay. What are you thinking?"

We cross the street, and I spot a crimson vase in a shop window and take a few steps in that direction before reconsidering.

"It would be good if one of us could accompany them to doctor appointments," she says. "It would help to have someone there to ask questions and keep us all informed. And Dad really needs to get out by himself more often. He's not going to do that unless one of us is there spending time with Mom."

"Okay."

"Plus, I think we could do some cooking and baking to help out. Dad is making all the meals on top of everything else."

I take a deep breath and sigh. "Let's take a break and stop in here," I suggest as we approach an ice cream shop. Maybe if we slow down, everything else will.

Sitting across the table from Denise with my bowl of chocolate chip ice cream, I'm struck by how different we are. She'll order a cup of herbal tea. I'll take the coffee. She likes tofu. I'm allergic to soy. Her hair is long and brown. Mine, short and blond. Her eyes are hazel. Mine are blue. Yet the resemblance is undeniable.

And there's a likeness to the context within which we seem to approach many of life's decisions. That's not to say we agree on everything (we don't), or that our experiences on this earth have been identical or even similar (they haven't). It's just that our frame of reference—shaped, molded, and shared in childhood—still remains a powerful influence on how we think. Not so surprising, I guess. Where you come from has a lot to do with where you're going.

"I know we've already got busy schedules," Denise says. Then she *does* order a cup of herbal tea. "It's hard to imagine squeezing in another thing alongside a full-time job. But I've got to find a way."

"We will."

Of course, it's easy to take all this sisterhood stuff for granted. I know I did until she moved to Seattle. Those were the years that made me think. Made me realize. Made me change.

I remember the day she called to say she was moving back from the West Coast. Ernie came running down the stairs to see why I was jumping up and down and shouting on the deck. And crying.

What could I say? Someone who'd been by my side ever since I could remember was coming back to me. And this time, I vowed, it would be different. I would be different. And I am.

And it looks like things are changing again. It would be easy to say that unlike when my youngest child moved out of the house, this latest change blindsided me. I never saw it coming. But is that really true?

For many of us, loosening the responsibilities on one side of the generational strand correlates with a tightening on the other. Our parents are getting older. Little by little, they're slowing down. That they'll need more help, care, and attention isn't a huge revelation. Perhaps, in my case, I was just looking the other way. I was thinking and hoping they wouldn't need me until sometime down the road. After I had a chance to catch my breath.

"I know this is a lot," Denise says as we pay our bill and step out into the sunlight.

"It is. I feel like, in a strange way, we're becoming parents to our parents."

The chilly wind picks up. Time to head back. Past the sweet scent of pastry at the bakery. The streets clogged with cars. The sidewalks bustling with pedestrians.

Two sisters out walking and talking. Talking and walking. Where we're heading this time, I'm not so sure. But I'm glad my sister is here by my side.

Home Sweet Home

"Did he really say that?" Ernie asks as we sit dumbfounded in our family room, recalling the meeting several years ago that catapulted us into a state of total detachment from our house.

"I'm afraid so," I say, sinking deeper into the couch.

At the time, the idea had seemed simple. What if we could hire someone to reimagine and reconfigure our home with creativity and vision—but hopefully not our entire life savings—and what if he could, in the process, visualize a way to alter the rotting windows, worn shingles, and sagging roof, and somehow magically transform it all into the shingle-style cottage of our dreams?

After we met with the architect several times; after we drove by houses he'd designed, just the kind we'd been dreaming of; after he surveyed our property; after we walked him through our house; after we plunked down a hefty deposit for reserving a spot on his schedule, he came back to us with a rough sketch and floor plan that got us excited about the possibilities. Right here on our own land!

No buying and selling. No moving and uprooting. No looking and comparing, negotiating and offering. Instant gratification, except, of course, for the year or so it would take to build. There was just one little catch. The house he imagined for us would be constructed directly in front of our existing home. Which begged the question: what would become of this one?

"Well," he had said in a solemn voice, staring down at the ground on the very spot where our amazing new dream house would be built. "After construction, when everything is done and you're all moved in, well, we would just blow it up."

Say what?

After more than twenty years of cleaning, painting, repainting, plumbing, wiring, rewiring, flood prevention, radon abatement, water purification, decorating, and redecorating, the prognosis was . . . . Could you repeat that, please? Did I hear you say . . . ?

Blow it up!

"Maybe that's why we haven't done anything these past few years. I think it's the architect's fault," Ernie laughs, shakes his head, and sighs.

"I think he might have even offended our house."

That explains the retaliation that's been going on all around us. The two windows that have been stuck closed for years are suddenly joined by half a dozen others precisely during the most sweltering August at the end of the hottest, most humid New England summer we can remember.

The expansive two-level deck, which was once adorned with flowerpots and white latticed chairs, the same deck that was the perfect garden setting for Denise and Claude's wedding, is now an official death trap, the boards warping and coming apart at the seams so badly that we must memorize our foot patterns on each stair to safely make our way into the backyard. The gutters are clogged with leaves. Heavy rains seep into the basement. The septic system gives out. And as if to put an exclamation point on the whole wretched situation, the mailbox keels over in the middle of the road, our letters and bills and flyers scattering all over our neighbor's yard.

"Now that Meredith is off at college, we've really got to do something here. The prudent thing would be to reshingle, reroof, patch things up, and make the most of what we have," Ernie says staring at the floor.

Over all these years, dreaming of The House became one of our favorite pastimes. We'd crisscrossed the region with realtors and popped in and out of open houses. We'd driven by grassy lots and slowed down every time we saw a "for sale" sign. We'd imagined ourselves in this tree-shaded colonial or that sun-drenched contemporary just a stone's throw from the beach. We'd been obsessed with the idea of the perfect house for years, but for some reason, we'd never actually found it. We'd just talked and dreamed and envisioned. And now we're going to do what? Settle?

"It's pretty sad," Ernie says. "All that talking and dreaming—maybe that's what's kept us from actually, well, living. We don't entertain anymore. We just meet friends at restaurants. It seems like we've just let go."

"Well, we've had a lot of other things going on. Work. Kids. Everything."

"Everyone has work, kids, everything going on, and they still seem to keep up with their homes."

"It doesn't really matter if they do or if they don't. We're the ones who are in this situation."

"Okay." I sink back into the couch. "What do you want to do?"

"I don't have any ideas."

This discussion is nothing new. We know the questions all too well. Should we renovate? Should we rebuild? How about a move? Maybe buy a lot. Maybe we should pack it all in and move to a condo in Florida, go all in on the white slacks and Lilly Pulitzer skirts, the golf clubs and full-on retirement thing.

But the answer never seems to come. We've analyzed The Great House Decision from every angle, weighing pros and cons, creating spreadsheets and elaborate diagrams. We think, we talk, we ponder—but that's as far as it goes.

We could blame our stasis on the architect. I'd like to do that. But that would be yet another way to kick the can down the road, to absolve ourselves from the consequences of our decisions, or in this case, our indecision. It's not the architect. But he has definitely added a new weapon to our arsenal in defense of the status quo. How can we justify getting the deck repaired, or the back steps rebuilt, or the windows replaced when one of the grand plans on the table right now is to blow our house to bits? Might as well blow our bank account to bits. Not a good idea at any time, but particularly destructive at this point in our lives when there are so many uncertainties. How much longer will we work? The clock is racing. We need to race, too.

In the meantime, I think we've become more and more attached to where we are, not just in this stuck place of indecision but also in the house itself. As so many things shift in our lives with Geoff all grown up and working in Boston and Meredith away at college in New York, it's hard to make yet another monumental change—this one of our own free will. I suspect that underneath it all, there's an emotional undertow that keeps us swimming in place, preventing us from climbing our way to new ground. But the reality is as clear as the paint that's chipping off the front door. We've got to do something soon! Very soon.

"So, let's solve this once and for all." Ernie shakes his head again. "We've got to figure this out now."

I sigh and look over at my husband running his hands through his dark hair, which is getting too long again. "You're right. It's time."

How do we get so stuck in life? How do we become so frozen in our tracks? We can't make a move. Not. One. Step. Forward. All we can manage is to go around and around in circles.

Maybe the better question is *why* do we get so stuck? Why is there no clear path, no turn right or left that emerges as a way out of the quagmire? And why can't we just take a leap of faith? Just do something. Anything. Wouldn't that be better than all the dithering?

And the best question of all is how do we get unstuck? Do we listen to reason or trust our instincts? Do we ask for advice or follow our hearts? Do we set a deadline or wait for inspiration? Or maybe we just get up off the couch, put one foot in front of the other, and start going. Start moving. Start living.

In the Yellow Kitchen

The recipe is the same as it has always been. Flour, sugar, baking powder, milk, butter, egg, baking soda. Two bananas ripened long past eating, soft and bruised fruit.

The kitchen has always been the same, too, at least as far back as my memory will take me. Impossibly yellow walls that match the countertops. A round table set in the center of a square room. Windows that peer out on an expanse of green yard punctuated by a white birdbath. A bulletin board hanging on the wall, pinned with greeting cards and invitations, photos of family and friends, and reminders of events and appointments, the stuff of life coaxed into a tidy tic-tac-toe pinned up for all to see.

My mother sits at the table tapping the wooden spoon I've handed her on the lip of the mixing bowl. I measure two cups of flour, a teaspoon of baking soda, and one of powder. She stirs them together, her eyes focused on her task, her right arm working hard. Once the powders are mixed, she taps the spoon on the bowl and looks up at me.

I glance over at the backsplash. It's fashioned from contact paper, yet surprisingly intact for something that transitory, painstakingly applied there decades ago by a teenager determined to leave her mark before setting out into the world. Little did the teenager know that her journey would take her past college, into marriage and out, and on to corporate positions and promotions until she ultimately reached a crossroads where what mattered more than any of it was another chance at love, another try at marriage, another opportunity to make her own home and family. There would be the birth of a son and that of a daughter, followed by a personal rebirth as a writer, all of it forever grounded by the family and home she came from, that *I* came from.

Carefully, almost tenderly, Mom mixes the softened stick of butter, a cup of sugar, one egg, two slushy bananas, and three tablespoons of milk. Despite how many times she has done this over the years, she looks surprised that there is yet another thing to add and then another. Despite how slowly she stirs the lumpy mixture, how deliberately each ingredient is added, she laughs and taps the wooden spoon on the silver bowl with childlike delight.

As I sit here with her, I realize there's something I took long ago from this woman, from this yellow kitchen, that I can rely on when all else fails. There's something folded into the measuring and the sifting, the mashing and the mixing, that I can bring with me. For in this ritual, in this unpredictable world, I will find warm assuredness that in precisely one hour, in a 350-degree oven, the results will always and forever be the same. The bread will rise. The air will swell with comfort. No matter where the kitchen, I can close my eyes and breathe in the familiar sweetness, and I am home.

She tells me about the group of people who gathered around this table a few days ago. I know this as I was there, summoned for a family meeting. But I don't let on to her. I don't want to get in the way of her enthusiasm for what she is saying. For what she is remembering. As it turns out, she doesn't recall who the people were or why they came together. What she does know is how much she enjoyed their company. "People like the yellow walls," Mom says. "They make you want to come here to my kitchen. They make you want to stay."

When did life sneak up behind us and play its awful trick, flip its switch and just like that, even if we're sitting in the kitchen in the house where we grew up, everything has changed? Suddenly, we've become the teachers, the leaders, or the ones who are supposed to know the recipe.

Or did we?

I look over at my mom. She's smiling in a contented way I've never seen before. It's as if she wants to tell me something but then thinks the better of it and hesitates as if I might already know. Is this woman sitting here so close to me, yet so far, expressing herself in a new and subtle way that requires me to pay more careful attention? Could it be that I'm mistaken about the shift in our roles, that some things do indeed remain true in this place that time has forgotten?

All morning I've been here in the kitchen with her, baking with her, and she is happy to help even though it's become harder. She finds delight in the moment, even though it's nothing new. She paints the walls of her world cheerful and bright, even as circumstances grow grim. She makes a point to share her joy with others, even if they're not paying attention.

But we're paying attention now. And to think we might have missed it. Another recipe passed down to us in the yellow kitchen.

Weighing In

Maybe I should have said no to the digital scale. From the moment our old one bled its red rust all over the white tiles of our bathroom floor and Ernie wanted to get a new state-of-the-art model, I knew it would be a mistake. But who was I to get in the way of progress?

With our sleek new scale, there is no more jiggling around to get in just the right position on top of it, to get at just the right angle to see it, to get that weekly reading I want, I need. Instead, there it is, the digital readout staring me in the face, its bold, black numbers precise and accurate to the tenth of a pound.

The battle goes back to a little girl who thought she was bright and pretty until she came of age in an awful way. Looking back on it now, I'm not sure which moment of shame came first.

Maybe it was the day after Halloween. During the night, somebody had left a message for me in shaving cream on the side of the house near my bedroom. FAT RITA. That's what it said. A trick-or-treat prank played by the neighborhood boys. A little something to let me know the crushes I had on some of them were in no way mutual, not even close. Dad tried washing away the insult with a garden hose only to discover the chemicals in the shaving cream had bonded with the red paint on our house, leaving a lasting impression. FAT RITA would stay there until the house could be repainted.

And then there was the picture-perfect summer's day when I was out exercising, trying to do something positive about what Mom referred to as my "healthy" look, peddling my bike up the long hill that led to our house, when a car packed with boys slowed down next to me to take a closer look. I was flattered. At long last, I was attracting some male attention. The new exercise plan must be working. Suddenly, a long arm shot out of the rear window and slapped some reality onto my backside. *"Fat ass!"* the boys hollered as the car sped off amid a chorus of laughter.

Or perhaps it was that illuminating day in high school gym class, this after spending eight years at a Catholic elementary school where the most physical activity we got was taking a walk at recess to a nearby brook where one of our faster classmates showed us how to smoke cigarettes. I still remember that high school gym, us girls lined up in our little blue shorts for a very public weigh-in in front of the stern Phys Ed teacher. Stern is putting it mildly. If she had been a drill sergeant in a Marine boot camp, she would not have been out of place. Looking for an advocate, I asked for her reassurance that the higher number I logged in on the scale was okay, that I was normal, just like the other girls. "Not in my book, honey!" she said in a booming voice that echoed throughout the gym. "You've got some work to do."

There were other times, other memories, many of which I would like to forget, but I can't. After shaping my young life in more ways than one, they still haunt me all these years later. Like many who struggle with extra pounds, my weight, and therefore my adolescence, had its ups and downs. Did it ever. Every summer during high school and college, thanks to the physical activity demanded by my waitress job and the bike ride to get there, I would slim down. I would *almost* like the way I looked. And then the cold weather would set in, and my days were spent sitting in classrooms and libraries and coffee shops studying and snacking. And snacking some more. Like a hibernating bear, I packed on the pounds. No matter what anyone said about beauty being only skin deep and personality being what matters, people's reactions to Summer Slim Rita were light-years away from their responses to Winter Weightier Rita. To say it was like night and day was an understatement. You could argue that my confidence soared when I was thinner and, of course, that was true. But on any given night out in the summer, I would be asked to dance, offered a drink, and pursued for my phone number. At any school dance or frat party during the winter, after all the couples had parted, I'd inevitably be one of the girls left behind, relegated to the small and damaged group gathered in the kitchen gorging on peanut butter and jelly sandwiches to assuage our disappointment. The message emblazoned on my psyche was clear: We like you for how you look, not who you are.

It should come as no surprise that I've carried this weight-consciousness thing along with me like a very large anchor wherever I've traveled. Sometimes it grows bigger and sometimes smaller, no pun intended. Whether I was shopping for just the right suit for a job interview, commuting sixty miles a day, putting in seventy-hour weeks at an ad agency, nine months pregnant, or trying on bathing suits before a Florida vacation, I was hyper-conscious of my body, super cautious of what I ate, and strictly monastic about exercise. In spite of it all, I'm proud to say that, for the most part, I'd managed to make peace with my body, finding a healthy balance of weight all year long.

But then the digital scale arrived, which was around the same time I found myself with no kids at home and a career up in the air. Given my competitive nature, I'm going to admit that maybe I've been a little obsessive about the whole weight thing.

If the competition every week is to beat the number on the scale from the previous week, well, you can see the problem. If I go lower one week, then lower again the next, eventually I'm going to find myself in uncharted territory. Maybe dangerous territory. And I know that. Rationally, I do.

But here's the thing.

When everything else is spiraling off in every direction; when my kids are miles away and no longer under my watchful eye; when I find myself longing to get back to my writing career but finding it easier said than done; when we're not sure we'll have enough money to live on should we decide to call it a day; when our house is falling apart and we can't figure out what to do with it; when my parents need more time and attention and so do my friends; well, this one small thing—big, bold numbers on a digital scale—gives me some reliability I'm not finding anywhere else in my life at the moment.

Struggling with your weight is a fierce battle that wages between your body and your mind, unleashing behavior that can cut you off from all sense, all logic. It's one thing to realize the struggle's roots are entangled deep in your psyche, perhaps scars from a childhood wound that never fully healed. It's quite another to use that insight to defeat a craving for chocolate cake, pepperoni pizza, or a bag of barbecue potato chips late at night when fatigue sets in and your defenses are down. Or to stop running too far and walking too much and going to the gym too often, all the while eating too little because some thought, some fractured shame from the past, got stuck in your head and just won't let go.

That's how it goes sometimes, and I know it's not good. I hear my husband, my kids, and several of my friends gently telling me that I look a little thin these days. I get that. And I do realize that I need to work on changing things, dialing back my attitude, my fastidiousness, my obsession with this part of my life.

And I will.

Talking about the struggle is a good first step. Sharing vulnerable moments and being honest about the challenges will help to turn them around. Because even though the numbers on the scale are cold, hard evidence that I'm in control, I see them for what they really are.

An illusion.

The Codependent Publicist

"How long has it been?" I pull up a chair and settle in across the table from Lisa at the bakery in Jamestown, warming my hands on the steaming mug of coffee.

"Maybe a year or two since we drove up to that author event in Providence together. Glad you reached out. I love this place." Lisa smiles as she stirs her tea.

"I've been reading about your upcoming writing workshop. Have a lot of people signed up?"

"More than I expected. And with all the authors I'm coaching, and the boys home from school, it's going to be a busy stretch."

"That's great!"

"So tell me what you've been up to since you stopped writing the column?"

I hesitate for a moment, flashing through the scenes in my head. Dropping Meredith off at NYU. Walking on the rocky beach. Running and thinking and running some more. Writing samples of a political column that wasn't right for me but took an editor from *The Washington Post* to make me realize it. Collaborating with another writer on a two-month project only to find we were heading in opposite directions.

"No decision yet. Honestly, I'm kind of lost."

"*Hmmm*," Lisa says as she takes a bite of her chocolate croissant. "I think I've got an idea for you."

I pull my chair a little closer.

"With your background in marketing and advertising, combined with your writing and journalism experience, you'd make a terrific book publicist."

Say what? Well, yes indeed. I guess I would.

How lucky I am! I've fallen headfirst into a new career opportunity. I didn't think. I didn't plan. I just went out for coffee with my friend the book coach and, as so often happens in life, one thing led to another.

Just like that, I'm on my way to becoming a book publicist. I'm following up on leads. I'm cranking out proposals. Before you know it, I've got clients! Just like when I had my marketing business only, instead of promoting products and services, I'm selling authors and their writing projects. I'm representing writers who need some help getting publicity, some assistance with articles and short stories and getting them placed.

"Hey, honey," Ernie says over the dinner that we're eating a little later than usual. "How was your day? Did you get a chance to write that essay you were telling me about?"

"Maybe tomorrow."

I keep telling myself this is too good to be true. Every day, I bounce out of bed with a renewed sense of purpose. I've got so much to do. Queries to write. Articles to edit. I'm working on getting placement and airtime for my clients. I'm working to get them noticed, quoted, and read so they can build their platforms. I'm working so that when their book projects are finished, when they're ready to contact agents and publishers, they've already established themselves as publishable experts in their respective fields whom readers listen to and want to hear more from. And that will help to boost their books in a big way.

The next night, Ernie is sweet not to mention that dinner is later. "I thought you were going to visit your mom today."

"Maybe tomorrow."

And I'm making money. Not a ton. Not like my marketing and advertising days when my clients were big-name companies with big-time budgets. These authors are regular people after all—doctors, therapists, lawyers, grandmothers, artists, people with expertise or a clever take on something. There's not much chance of getting a big consulting fee. So I'm charging a modest one. Just to get started, I tell myself.

"Did you get a chance to go to the market? Maybe we should just get takeout tonight," Ernie says a few days later.

All of a sudden, I'm so busy. With the demands of my new clients on top of the bookkeeping I do for Ernie's business, and all the behind-the-scenes things I do to keep this house and family up and running, it feels like, well, normal. It fits like a pair of old Sauconys that I just can't throw away. It keeps me going at the same frenetic pace I've been running at ever since Ernie and I got married, bought this house, and launched two businesses while raising our kids.

The thing is, I'm getting up earlier and earlier. I'm not wasting a minute. I'm one of the most efficient people on the planet, yet I'm having trouble keeping up. Maybe this is just how life is. It's certainly how it was all those years. So why did I think that when Meredith left for college, I'd be heading for something new, something wondrous and inspiring and uplifting?

"You seem so frazzled lately." Ernie again. "It's nice to have the extra money, but you don't seem like yourself."

How can he see right through me?

The truth is, at least right now, we don't need the money I'm earning from this publicity business. I'm not going to lie, it's nice to make it. It helps us to do a few things that we might not otherwise. And I like the sense of purpose and pride that earning again brings to me, far more familiar and comforting than being lost in the great big emptiness that my life has become. And yet . . .

How do we make meaningful changes in our lives if we're not willing to get uncomfortable? How do we explore who it is we truly are and what kind of life we actually want if we cling to the familiar? Why do we run away like scared rabbits from having all the time in the world and burrow right back into our holes, where we never have enough time in the day? Why do we resist having nothing to do, and, at a moment's notice, dive headfirst into doing nothing but doing?

We can't just quit. We can't just stop. We can't just think and listen and consider.

Or can we?

Our Winter Vacation

Ernie and I are braving the blustery wind as we stand on the platform at the train station in nearby Kingston, eagerly anticipating Meredith's arrival. Lizzie is here with us, too. She knows who's coming. Her tail can't wag fast enough.

With more bags than you'd think anyone could possibly handle, a young woman strides toward us in a bright red coat and brown leather boots. She looks like our daughter, only different. Is it the way she walks? Did she get new clothes? Is she taller? I can't be sure it's really her until she gets closer, drops her bags, and bends down to greet her faithful friend, who whimpers with joy. Meredith hugs her dad and me and then gets down to the business at hand. It's the third week of December, after all.

"When are we getting the tree?"

The next day finds us in Kingston again, which also happens to be the home of our favorite tree farm. We make our way from the parking lot down to the rows of Christmas trees, the scent of pine filling the cold air. "How about this one?" I ask, stopping at a balsam fir that seems about right for our dining room.

"Not full enough," says Ernie.

"Not tall enough," says Meredith.

We head for another section of the farm to check out the white pines. The December sun proves to be ineffective in the north wind.

"I bet we'll find The Perfect Tree faster this year," I say. "We're not going to last long out here."

One of us disagrees. Lizzie is having the time of her life sniffing tufts of grass and fallen branches, running this way and that, and greeting every tree shopper who happens to come along.

"This is late for us to be getting a tree," Ernie says. Then he looks over at our daughter. "But no way would we have come here without you."

Meredith has always loved everything about Christmas. The presents. The decorations. The baking. The dinners. The guests. The parties. And as she's grown older, she's taken an active role in helping to make it all happen. She especially enjoys decking out our house, transforming every corner into a festive celebration. When we finally bring home The Perfect Tree later that day, she gets busy right away with the ornaments and the bows, the wreaths and the laurel. "Everything has to stay up until after I go back to New York," she says with a smile. But I don't think she's kidding.

Every day for the better part of six weeks, Meredith is here with us. I can sit in my office and hear her downstairs, waking up, rustling around, running water, opening cabinets, pouring milk, clattering, and chattering to her faithful breakfast companion. I can come down whenever I feel like it and there she is, perched on the couch, book in her lap, phone in her hand, computer on the table, Lizzie curled up at her feet. On most mornings, I walk into a new plan brewing, a new scheme rising, and a new day dawning.

Gone are the strange order and odd predictability of the days that had spooled out in front of me like some foreign film during her first semester away at college. House quiet. Hours long. Intentions cloudy. Identity uncertain. Day by day, I had gone about the hard, uncomfortable, and sometimes painful business of finding myself. Digging up the forgotten pieces. Discovering new ones. Trying them on, this way and that.

But now she's back, and I'm back to where we both belonged for so many years, as if the past semester never happened.

How is this possible? It's as if we parents never say long goodbyes to our kids. When they come back, everything seems the same as it always was. There's no adjustment necessary. No assembly required. Everything feels right. Even better than that.

Even The Perfect Tree seems more resplendent than those of years gone by, somehow bigger and taller, with shinier ornaments and more twinkling lights that set the merry mood. Our guests laugh more and linger longer. Even after the holidays.

But despite all the festivities, our winter break also turns out to be a time of reflection and discovery. With a semester of college under her belt, Meredith has uncovered new insights and revelations about herself. As for me, I'm here to listen, to share, and to sometimes guide her. How lucky I am she is so close.

Until suddenly, once again, she is so far.

What began on the platform of the Kingston train station, stretching out over cold days and even colder nights, has come to a close. Just like that. One long trip to New York City with the car packed to the hilt and it's over. I walk back into our house, and it feels strange. Empty. All over again.

This morning, I step into her room and the emptiness unexpectedly greets me. The books are gone from her shelves. The laptop is missing from her desk. The quilt on her bed is neat and tidy. No one is here rustling around, making breakfast, or talking to the dog. All I hear is the hollow patter of my own footsteps on the wooden floor, and a long sigh from Lizzie curled up in the corner, no doubt hoping her buddy will burst through the door and all the lively activity that has amused us for these past weeks will carry on as if nothing has happened. But something *has* happened. For once again, the door is closed, leaving me to find my way in this new reality that feels so different, so difficult to describe.

I miss Meredith. But I know, too, that she needs the separation. The distance. The gentle nudge to go out into the world and find herself. And as it turns out, I need the same.

I feel sad.

And I feel happy.

Bliss for the Taking

"You must have enjoyed having your daughter home." That's what she said, my neighbor Jackie standing there near my driveway, braving the icy wind to walk her dogs. A little wisdom offered up on a winter's morning. And you know what? I'm taking it. That's what's been missing around here. Joy. And let it begin with me.

I know there are challenges.

Case in point: When Meredith came home from college for the holidays, she brought a whole suitcase filled with things she needed to sort through. That's not unexpected. On any given road, there are ups and downs, twists and turns. And when that road happens to run through New York City, where you're a teenager living on your own for the first time, well, it can all get overwhelming.

We all know something about overwhelming. It comes along all too often with daily experience. On the one hand, there are the mundane tasks that never end: laundry, cooking, dishes, cleaning, errands, and that sort of thing. Things that get completed for the moment and then, before there's a chance to relax and enjoy the satisfaction of a job well done, there they are, right back at us, demanding to be done over and over and over again.

Then we add in work, the interminable need to make a living, in addition to all the other non-paying effort required for raising a family, maintaining relationships, and keeping a home. We go to the office. We get paid. For a fleeting moment, we've got a check in our hands, a positive balance in our bank account, and then, in the blink of an eye, we start paying bills and more bills, and just like that, we're right back where we started by the end of the month.

There are unforeseen landmines, of course. We get hurt. We get sick. We lose our jobs. We lose our way. We're out of money. We're out of time. We make mistakes. We fix them, or so we try. There is nothing new here. This is the way it's been going for most of us, more or less, since we stopped playing house and moved into a real one, since we stopped pretending to be grown up because incredibly, we found ourselves becoming more like our parents than we ever thought possible. Adulthood, when we think of it this way—and I'll admit I often do—can be oh so overwhelming. But then there's Jackie. She's out there on a freezing morning with the north wind whipping at her face, all bundled up in her bright pink parka, walking her two yellow Labradors, and she's smiling at me.

"You must have enjoyed having your daughter home."

Here's a thought. What if we try something different? What if we just keep doing what we've been doing but infuse a little joy into every step along the way? What if we take a cue from the surprise gift for me that Geoff brought home last week, a red sparkly sleeve that fits snugly around my takeout cup so that drinking coffee suddenly becomes a celebration, a glittering break in the day to relax and enjoy? What if we stay in the moment instead of racing fast and furious into the unknowable days and weeks and years ahead? What if we keep smiles that come in pink parkas and thoughtfulness decked out in sparkling red and all the other colorful blessings of our days at the center of our consciousness and learn to look through this brighter lens?

And there it is, plain as day. My New Year's resolution: *Be joyful!*

Find the fun and good and happiness in every moment and embrace it. Forget all the hoping for the ideal situation, all the waiting for the perfect moment, all the searching for the unobstructed stretch of road ahead. What if it never comes? What if we never find it? What if things get worse? What if these are, like the song says, the good old days?

Why not enjoy this time, these moments, this work, these chores, this family, those friends? Why not make the most of the pile of fresh-smelling towels that needs to be folded, the disco tune that comes on the radio when we're stuck in traffic, or the banana bread that gets left in the oven a bit too long but tastes pretty good with an extra layer of crust? Well, there it is then. A new life philosophy inspired by my neighbor Jackie, out walking her dogs in the frigid morning.

I will find my bliss. I will look for it in my work, in my marriage, in my family, in my friendships, my moments, my days, the quiet, the crowd, my house and all its shortcomings, a talk with a neighbor in an icy driveway, a freshman who came home for the holidays but had to go back, a cup of coffee decked out in sparkling red, and the son who was thoughtful to give it to me just because. Just because we're here. Just because we're alive. Just because we can walk and smile and listen and learn and change.

Find the joy! Find the happy! As it turns out, it's been there all along, just waiting for me, waiting for us.

Bliss for the taking.

A Midwinter's Night Out

I push myself out the door and into the frigid darkness, shivering my way to the garage only to settle into the cold car. Struggling to get a grip on the steering wheel with my mittens, I head down the road, hoping the heat will kick in soon, and all I can think of is this: My friend Kathy must have been born in January for a reason. A very good reason. That would be to get us out of the house for Girls' Night during the one time of year when we're already spent in every way—physically, emotionally, and financially. But it's her birthday, and she's a terrific friend. So cold or no cold, I'm going out. We're going out.

My gift will hopefully inspire a theme for the season. I chose for her three candles in bright spring colors and a book by Anna Quindlen, *Lots of Candles, Plenty of Cake*. Although I never could have predicted it, the poignant memoir about this time in our lives is a harbinger of what's in store for us this evening.

At our favorite pub, the fireplace aglow, settling into a glass of chardonnay with two friends that I grew up with through our years at Catholic school, I'm already glad we made it here on this winter's night. We chatter about the holidays, exchange updates on our kids and families, and offer condolences to Carol on her aunt's recent passing. We ask about Kathy's son's upcoming wedding, get the latest news about Carol's photography, and discuss my parents' health. We are caught up. Or so we think.

Sometime in between our salads and the main course, Carol goes for it, sharing the news she's been holding back from Kathy for many months, waiting for the right time, the right place, the right mood. I know what's coming. I have known for a while now. Still, I brace myself.

"I got divorced," Carol says, voice steady, eyes on Kathy. "I didn't tell you because he didn't want anyone to know at first."

Kathy looks startled for a beat. Then she takes a deep breath, glances around the room for a moment, and returns her gaze to Carol. "What happened?"

"Long story, but he was doing some things I just couldn't live with. It really became a problem."

Before Kathy can respond, Carol charges ahead. "I'm doing much better than I was. I'm dating again." Oh, God, I think. She's really going for it. Yes indeed, she is.

Carol reaches into her pocket for her phone and scrolls to a photo of the new love of her life. She reaches across the table to show us the person she's been spending more and more time with, the one who's helping her get a smile back on her face.

She tells us her name.

To be honest, it's taken me some time to digest the surprising news. My best friend, who I thought was one way all her life, is now dating a woman. Not that I have a problem with that. I don't. It was just a bit shocking at first, this suddenly sharp turn she has taken. But if it makes her happy—and it sure seems to—I'm totally on board.

I can only hope Kathy will feel the same way. Especially since she's being put on the spot. Right here. Right now.

Kathy takes a long drink of merlot, staring down at her glass. A puzzled expression crosses her eyes but quickly fades. "I hope he's okay," she says. "He's a good guy underneath it all. He had a tough childhood, so that makes it hard. And yes, Carol, you have really surprised me this time, that's for sure. But the bottom line is this: I love you. I just want you to be happy."

"I am!"

Kathy goes on. "This time of our lives, when our kids are moving out and getting married, when our parents are ill or passing on, well, life is just coming at us like a freight train. Think about it. What do we have left? Thirty years, if we're lucky. Maybe twenty. I've just decided to make the most of them, to go after what I want and be happy."

She tells us she went skiing on her birthday earlier in the week. Her husband couldn't take the day off from work. So she packed her skis into the car and went by herself. And had a great time. By herself.

That's the same attitude that has inspired her recent travels to Italy and California with another trip planned to Spain next fall. "I've always wanted to travel. No more wanting. No more waiting. I'm going. So if Carol is happy, that's what matters."

"I want to be, too," I say, surprising myself as the words escape my lips. "I'm worried about my parents. I'm not sure what to do about my career, our house, or anything! So much coming at me."

"This is a hard time for you," Kathy says. "You're in a difficult place. You're being stretched in one direction and squeezed in another. That's what happens at our age, especially in our generation. But try to take the time to do the things that will make you happy in spite of it all. Take that walk if it ever warms up enough. Go out to dinner with Ernie. Keep in mind this is your life. Your one and only one."

Take the time to do the things that will make you happy. In spite of it all.

Keep in mind this is your life. Your one and only one.

It's Kathy's birthday. But somehow it ends up that, on this particular Girls' Night, when we've come out on this bitterly frigid evening with presents to celebrate her day, it's Kathy who's given us the real gift.

Fighting Nemo

t's Friday evening during the second semester of our newfound couplehood, and I'm brewing coffee. I tell Ernie I'm doing this because I bought a new flavor at the market, snickerdoodle, or something like that, and I can't wait to try it. That's not the truth. The real reason I'm making coffee at 6:30 on a Friday evening is because I have a strong suspicion this will be my last cup for a while. Maybe days.

Nemo has arrived.

A few hours later, a strong gust of wind shuts us down. We have no lights, no refrigerator, no oven, no dishwasher, no running water, no washer, no dryer, no television, and no heat! All of the conveniences and pleasures we take for granted have gone dark. We've entered into a new zone. Welcome to survival, baby!

We already know the heat will become the major problem on this blustery February weekend as Blizzard Nemo bears down on us. Despite the early hour, Ernie and I do what anyone without a fireplace, a wood stove, or a generator would do under the circumstances. We pile every blanket we've got onto our bed, hunker down for the night, and hope for the best.

White morning dawns, and the temperature inside our house is plummeting. Quickly. We've got our hands full shoveling our way from the front door to the garage in the unlikely event we're ever able to get out of here. Listening to the updates on the radio confirms that's not likely to happen anytime soon. There's a travel ban. Emergency vehicles only. Not that it matters. There's got to be at least three feet out there and more heading our way soon.

Is it possible for your brain to actually go numb? The colder it gets in here, fifty-two degrees according to the thermometer in the kitchen, the less connected and coherent my thinking becomes. This is not helpful. This is not helpful at all. I need to stay sharp. I've got a lot to figure out.

First and foremost are Mom and Dad. They live in Middletown, about twenty miles away, but today it might as well be twenty thousand. A call there confirms what I already feared. They're not doing well. They've got no electricity, no heat, no help, and no way out. They won't be able to hold on much longer.

"We should have gotten a generator. I've been telling you that for years," Ernie says. "Even if we could get your parents, where are we supposed to take them?"

"We don't have a generator because we haven't decided what we're doing about the house."

"Meanwhile, we've got blizzards and no heat!"

"Maybe Denise and Claude are having better luck."

Ernie and I spend the morning shoveling and shivering, venturing outside only to quickly retreat and try warming up under blankets while listening to Operation Snowball on the radio. I sure could use a cup of coffee.

Around noon, the governor announces an exception to the travel ban for those without heat who could be in danger. That would be my parents. We switch off the radio, pull on our coats, and make our way out to the Land Rover. One way or another, we're breaking out of here.

Our rescue mission energizes our cold bodies. Suddenly, we're transformed into three warriors fighting our way through the storm, climbing into the car with our faithful Lizzie eagerly perched in the back. Armed with our cell phones, ice scrapers, and a shovel, we hope for the best as we barrel out into the white wilderness, our car somehow forging through. We stop at the end of the driveway to shovel the giant pile of ice and snow that the plows have left there. We get it down as much as we can. Back in the car, Ernie guns it. The wheels spin, he shifts gears, and he slams the gas pedal.

"Hang on! We're busting out!" he says, a big grin on his face. And just like that, we're free. Even better, we've got heat!

It's not good out here.

Snow drifts as high as a house. Fallen branches create a brown-and-white obstacle course in front of us. Patches of ice hide in waiting to slip us up. Other than the plows and a few emergency vehicles, at least we've got the road to ourselves. Slowly but surely, we make our way to my parents' house. And from the look on Dad's face as he peers out the garage door when we arrive, we're not a minute too soon.

He stands there shivering as Ernie and I take turns shoveling a pathway from the road to the house through what I now estimate to be at least four feet of white stuff in some places.

"Hang on, Dad! We're coming!"

We make it to the door and then form a human train, Mom's arms wrapped snugly around my waist to keep her steady on the slippery path. Step by step by step, we finally make it back to the warmth and safety of our car. My parents begin thawing out.

"It would be nice to get some coffee," Mom says. I couldn't agree more. But there are no restaurants open. How could there be?

We drive about thirty miles or so, a trek that takes us close to two hours, to Denise and Claude's house, where, for some reason or another, our family's luck has held out and the electricity has remained on. There, my parents will spend the night and maybe longer until their power returns. My sister invites Ernie and me to join them, but with the dog and all, we fear it will be too much. We thank them and drive away with no idea what we're going to do, though we know we'll figure something out. After all, that's what we've been doing ever since the first icy winds of Nemo blew our way. Figuring something out.

What is it about us human beings? Why do we tend to go around living our lives, only tapping into a small percentage of our potential? We're all too quick to underestimate ourselves, to cut ourselves short, when the truth is that we've got far more capacity than we believe. We possess many more talents and resources than we realize, and yet we go about our days utilizing only a tiny portion of our power and strength.

Until the unthinkable happens. We get fired from our job. We get divorced. We get transferred across the country and have to re-create our lives. Or maybe we're sitting in our family room on a perfectly fine Friday evening in February and we get slammed by a blizzard that shuts everything down. That's when we're forced to get up off the couch and shift into a higher gear. And we do! We rise to the occasion, stretch in ways we never thought possible, and use our dormant brains to figure something out.

For us, the next something turns out to be an extended-stay motel about fifteen miles from home. Not only do they have power, but they also welcome pets! And happen to be near a Dunkin' Donuts where the lights are actually on.

Once we're inside, the guy at the counter tells us they opened just five minutes ago, and they have nothing to sell yet. No donuts. No muffins. And no coffee!

But at this point, believe me, we don't care. We go back to the motel, content to sprawl out on the big bed with our warm dog and some pretzels, bread, and peanut butter that we bought at an open convenience store across the street. We're safe. We've got heat, something to eat, and even a TV! What more could we want?

For this one time, the coffee can wait.

Downward-Facing Mom and Dancer Dad

Sunlight filters through the grand windows, flickering on mirrors and pink walls, filling the studio with a rosy glow. Our circle forms, our chatter quiets, we sit straight and tall on our mats, and we let the yoga begin.

Truth to tell, I find this new Monday evening ritual to be difficult. Despite thinking I'm in fairly good shape, my very first class was illuminating. Running does not make a body flexible. At least, not mine. Quite the contrary. After that first class, I stumbled down the stairs from the studio with a pounding headache, most likely brought on from too much time in downward-facing dog, too much blood rushing to my brain, too many thoughts racing into the stillness I'd been hoping to find. Never again, I vowed.

But here I am.

When I look at the others in the group, many younger than I am, some dancers, and nearly all so much more flexible than me, I feel discouraged. But then, I am heartened by our instructor's words: "Move at your own pace. Find your edge. Trust in your body."

And whatever you do, don't look in the mirror! One glance confirms what I fear. When everyone else squats low to the ground, I'm flailing. When their backs are straight as boards, mine is round and curved. When they bend low, their heads touching the floor, well, *never mind*. Better just to close my eyes. Go inside myself. Move at my own pace. Trust in my body.

My practice is better this way, I think, concentrating on my own strengths and weaknesses instead of giving in to my competitive nature. I decide on following the instructor's advice and dedicate Monday evenings to my own journey, gently and lovingly testing the limits of my flexibility, my strength, and my balance. And if I stay with it long enough, I'm hoping for improvement to come in incremental ways, small movements that perhaps no one else will notice. Not the others in the class. Not even the teacher. Just me.

My reverie is suddenly interrupted by grunting and groaning coming from the mat next to me. I look over at Ernie, who decided to come along with me this evening for another marital adventure, another exploration of who we're becoming now that the kids are gone, this one spent twisting and turning in ways I never thought possible. I follow his gaze to the opposite side of the circle, where he's fixated on a man across from us on a blue mat. Did I mention the guy is a dancer? And at least a few decades younger.

"Yoga is a solo journey, a trek to the innermost corners of our bodies, our minds, and our spirits." That's what our instructor is saying. That's what I've been telling myself.

No matter. In some parts of our circle, in fact, right there on the mat next to me, it's game on. When Dancer Guy moves into an impossible pose, somehow balancing the weight of his extraordinarily muscular body on his two hands, Ernie is right there extending his limbs in directions that defy not only gravity but all common sense. When Dancer Guy launches into a perfect shoulder stand, the feet of the man I married reach for the sky. His legs akimbo, sweat pouring down in buckets, he mutters under his breath.

Stay focused, I tell myself. Stay centered. I try concentrating on my foot placement for warrior two, standing tall, stretching the side of my body, and reaching for the front and the back of the room with my arms.

But the warrior on the mat next to me—the husband I'm getting reacquainted with after all these years—is reaching for new heights. As the instructor guides us into half splits, apparently half is not nearly enough for someone I know and love. Stretch. Grunt. Stretch. Groan. Stretch, stretch, stretch. *Ouch!*

And so it goes, pose after pose, until we reach the close of what's turned out to be, for some of us, a surprisingly competitive class. Perhaps more surprising is that I'm not the one feeling that familiar fire, that need to outperform, to exceed and excel.

Is it possible that a weekly commitment to the poses and the practice can somehow help to smooth out the edges, and soften the intensity? Is it possible that staying centered in the present moment can teach a new state of being? A new way of accepting and trusting and letting go?

Finally, we allow our tired bodies to collapse on our mats, lying flat on our backs with our arms and legs extended in shavasana. We are quiet and still, grateful for this time to relax and reflect. We are content and satisfied, grateful for this moment to allow all the good work we've done to settle into our bodies. And one wife lying here is amused and relieved, grateful for this happy report from Monday night yoga. No major injuries were sustained.

Except, perhaps, to someone's ego.

An Asteroid Hits at Astor Place

On a weekend morning with any luck, we can make it from our home in Rhode Island to Meredith's place in Manhattan in three hours. Even though we've made the trip many times, I'm still fascinated by the gradual shift in scenery outside our windows—how the miles carry us from our rural island, where the most exciting thing to happen is the occasional deer darting in front of our car to a city forever on the edge of chaos. Yellow taxis, red stoplights, neon flashing all around. Sirens blaring, brakes screeching, a soulful saxophone serenading passersby. Shoppers shopping, bikers biking, buses, trucks, and vans jockeying for position. Salty pretzels, fresh fruit, spicy sausages sizzling on every corner. Protesters shouting, police gathering, pedestrians caught up in the impending storm.

But early on this Sunday morning, in the city that never sleeps, Ernie and I are surprised to find ourselves seemingly alone when we leave our hotel at dawn. Our walk takes us down deserted sidewalks where we can cross the streets at will. No cars. No pedestrians. No hustle. No bustle. Just the two of us and several homeless people sleeping on a sheet of cardboard on top of the subway grates.

In the cold stillness, we find our way to a Starbucks in the center of a traffic island in the East Village. Perched in a window seat looking out at the city waking up all around us, with large coffees in our hands, the chilly air in our lungs, and the brisk walk settling into our legs, everything in the world suddenly seems possible. We sit in silence, taking in the moment; the grinding of coffee beans the only sound as baristas prepare for the customers that surely will come through the doors soon, seeking warmth and comfort.

A sign in the distance for Cooper Union takes us down roads not traveled. "What would have happened if I'd gone to college in New York?" I ask, staring out at the cloudless blue sky. "Where would I be now if, all those years ago, I had realized how much I love writing and journalism, if my career had taken another turn?" If this. If that. If.

As fun as it is to imagine all the unsung possibilities, the *if onlys*, the *what might have beens*, here I sit, at the age that I am, with so much on my mind and in my heart that I want to share. Where could my path lead me now when I have far fewer miles left in front of me? Where could I actually go? And then, it comes. The epiphany. The inspiration that has eluded me for all these months. Maybe years. In this moment, it's so simple. So obvious. And yet, incredibly moving and monumental.

It reminds me of a dream that came to me last summer, during the heat of a humid August morning when I woke up damp, my cheeks clinging to the pillowcase, and my dear Auntie Gert's voice ringing in my ears.

She was so beautiful and amazingly talented. Yet practical and down to earth. And very outspoken! When I got married the second time, she pulled Ernie aside and said, "If you hurt my niece, you'll have me to deal with!" Even though she was half his size, he did not take her stern warning lightly.

In the dream, I was sweating. What should I do? How could I bring my stalled career back to life? I didn't know. But Auntie Gert did. "If you want to be a writer, then write." That's what she said.

If you want to be a writer, then write!

Sitting here with Ernie, sipping coffee, gazing out over the city and the life that isn't mine but could be our daughter's, I finally see. It's been staring me in the face all this time, somehow floating just beyond my vision. From this point on, there will be no more clients. No more publicity. No more editing. No more marketing or advertising or research. No more dithering or distractions or indecision. No more excuses. Nothing except two simple words.

Just. Write.

Get up every day and pour myself into my writing. Get to the page early, leave the house or stay in the house before anything or anyone gets in the way. Write about all the things on my mind and in my heart. Write about the journey I've been on. Tell the truth about what's happening outside and in, and hopefully make some sense of it all along the way. Get it down. Get it all down. Don't worry about what's going to happen, whether my words will make their way to readers, whether anyone besides me will ever hear what I have to say.

Just. Write.

Don't outline. Don't plot. Don't think about what's marketable and what's not. Just embrace the process, make the commitment, sift through the sand, and uncover the bones, as Stephen King likes to say. Have faith that the ideas will come. The words will follow. Allow myself, for perhaps the first time, to take a deep dive into who I really am at the core and let it rip. Dare to find my truth. And let it go.

Just. Write.

Have you ever experienced one of those moments of sparkling clarity when something you've been struggling to solve twists around in your head and becomes suddenly and surprisingly simple? The storm clouds have parted, the skies have cleared, and you're left standing there with your mouth wide open, staring at the revelation that just hit you out of the blue, filling you with joy and awe and gratitude.

"I need to find something," I say to Ernie, waving my hands excitedly as we're getting ready to leave. "Something. Anything. A brochure, a napkin, some symbol, some talisman to help me remember this moment. A little something to hang on to during those moments of doubt that will surely follow."

"Let's go look," Ernie says as we get up from our cozy perch by the window.

We circle back into the line that's now forming for coffee, looking to find something, some small validation that on this winter morning in a Starbucks in New York City, my eyes and my heart have been opened. And there it is! A mug. A stark black cup, the only one of its kind that I can see, sitting high atop a display of Special Reserve coffee. And in the center of the mug, two small symbols. A star. And an *R* for Rita. I'm certain. Or maybe, Reets, the nickname that's stayed with me since high school. That mug has to be it!

"Let me buy it for you, honey," Ernie says.

I hug him tightly and then tuck the mug into my bag. I will take it home and put it in my office where I can see it every day, so that no matter what else should come my way, I'll remember this morning. I will. And the message from my aunt that I heard in a dream, the path ahead I now can see so clearly.

Just. Write.

Emergency, Just a Phone Call Away

Beads of sweat trickle down my forehead. As I stand at the kitchen counter chopping green beans, I look over at Ernie emptying the dishwasher. "It's way too hot for entertaining," I say.

"You're telling me." He pulls his sweaty T-shirt away from his chest.

"What strange weather for this time of year! I just thought it would be nice to get the family together for Easter before Meredith goes back to New York."

"I don't think we've seen Geoff since Christmas. I can't believe he's been working in Boston for a year already. Where does the time go?"

I shift my attention to mixing the ingredients for Amish cocoa squares, one of my favorite desserts. The thought of turning on the oven to bake them, however, is not so appealing.

"I'm going to bring up a fan from the basement," Ernie says. Before he heads down the stairs, he wipes his brow and says, "I know the first thing on my list if we renovate. This is no way to live."

In the middle of my mixing, the phone in the family room rings. I quickly rinse my hands and hurry over to pick it up. Dad's voice is strained. I can't quite make out what he's saying. Something about bleeding. Dizziness. The emergency room. Suddenly, our party preparations screech to a halt. Ernie and I rush out the door and head to the hospital.

As Ernie drives over the Newport Bridge, I call Geoff and Meredith, who had gone out to do some errands. I ask them to call Denise and Claude. "Nana had to go to the hospital. We're on our way there now."

We make it to the emergency room and look for my mother stretched out on a bed. But we find her in the hallway, sitting uncomfortably on a metal chair, not sure of where she is, or what's going on. "Where's Dad?" I ask. She points to a nearby room.

"Dad!" Ernie and I peer into the room to find my father lying in the bed. "What happened?"

While we sit there waiting for the doctor, I can't help thinking how we really never know what we're going to be doing from one minute to the next. We think we know. We believe we do. We trick ourselves into assuming we have control over the course of our days. That's why we put so much time and effort into making elaborate plans, scheduling our waking hours down to the minute, plotting our activities in great detail in our planners, our calendars, even our watches. It's as if documenting our intentions will ensure that they will happen without interference. It's as if we believe that our plans will somehow hold back the unpredictable tide that can wash up at any moment onto the shores of our lives.

Life's inevitable unpredictability is a good thought to hold on to as they move Dad to another room, where he will stay overnight for observation. And then, as we soon learn, for a few more days for tests.

Denise and I quickly come up with a plan to take shifts staying with Mom for the next few days or however long it might be. And just like that, there's no family party, no shopping for spring clothes with Meredith, no leisurely days spent with Geoff, who has taken some time off from work. But I'm learning to roll with whatever comes my way, to soften my will, and adapt to whatever's needed of me in the moment. It's not easy, but it's essential. Especially now.

And then comes the good news. The bleeding and dizziness were caused by a change in Dad's heart medication. A different prescription quickly corrects the problem. Four days later, I'm standing outside the hospital doors with him and Mom, walking them to their car, where Dad is only too happy to get back into the driver's seat.

I, too, am happy to get into my car and drive back to my house and life, knowing my parents are okay.

For the moment.

Make This a Good Hair Day

Friday morning dawns, and I'm up before the sun. Not to work. Not to run or hit the gym. Not for a doctor's appointment, to help my parents, to go to the market, or to do anything that's even remotely responsible or necessary. Quite the contrary. I'm up early and driving nearly thirty miles to Providence, to a place where I started going when I used to work in the city.

When I enter the salon, Tammy, one of the owners, the reason I've been coming here for so many years, walks over and greets me. She's the one who's taken me from the twenty-something advertising executive who sprayed her hair with Sun-In to a more natural and healthier-looking blond. "Good to see you, Rita. Glad you were able to get an appointment with Sia."

"So, what's the occasion?" Sia asks as she ushers me back to her station, fastening the ties of the long black smock around my neck. She's able to do with a blow dryer what I never could—tame the dry and coarse hair my college boyfriend once referred to as "bushy" into soft, silky strands. "Big plans for the weekend?"

"I knew you'd ask," I say, settling into the chair as Sia massages some oil into my scalp.

"Well, you're not getting a cut or foils today. Just a blow dry, right?"

"It's an idea that popped into my head. I can never make my hair look as nice as you do."

Sia takes me over to the sink. I lean back in the chair, and she starts rinsing my hair. The warm water soothes the tension in my neck.

"I know it's indulgent. Kind of extravagant," I say.

"You deserve it, Rita. You're always doing so much for everyone. Just sit back and enjoy."

I take a deep breath and let her words sink in as the sweet coconut-scented suds soak into my hair.

"So, what *are* you doing this weekend?"

"Not much. I might make my yoga class this evening. Maybe stop somewhere for takeout with Ernie and kick back to watch a ballgame on TV."

"That sounds relaxing."

"What about you?"

"I might go out with a friend tomorrow night. And I'm thinking of tackling one of the cleaning projects around the house that always eludes me during the week."

"Yeah, I have a lot of those, too."

I walk back to Sia's station and settle into the chair. I smile in the mirror at her as she takes the towel from my head.

"It's funny, Sia. Now that I think about it, I've got no special plans. No plans at all. Just a weekend of relaxing with Ernie. And you know something? As the days and months without the kids go by, I'm finding that's what I like best."

Even though Sia is totally on board with my indulgent morning, there's someone who doesn't approve. Maybe you know her. Maybe she talks to you, too. I don't know where The Other Voice came from, but I've known her for a long time. Perhaps we met when I was talking during class in first grade and the nuns washed my mouth out with soap.

Ever since those early years, The Other Voice has been quick to interrupt my thoughts with her incessant messages. "You've got to get As. Act like the other girls. Look in the mirror. Get on the scale. Did you hear those boys jeering at you?"

All these years later, she still tries stirring up trouble. Whenever I do a little something for myself, there she is, The Other Voice. "You should be home cleaning the house," she says. "Washing clothes. Making calls. Paying bills. What about your writing? Where has your ambition gone?"

My ambition is just fine, thanks for asking. In fact, it's better now that my hair is clean and shiny, and I feel relaxed and happy having done something nice for myself.

Maybe you've discovered this, too. That it's easier to talk back now that we understand what happens when we don't make time for ourselves, especially when we're in the middle of a busy stretch or under a lot of stress. These are the times when we need to pay attention to ourselves even more than usual. Even if it's difficult to find the time. And if we're honest, when isn't it?

Pat, my therapist at the time of my divorce, taught me this many years ago when I was a single mom with an energetic son, a burgeoning business, and a sixty-mile-a-day commute. I needed help, and even though the once-a-week counseling sessions were tough to fit into my schedule, Pat also assigned homework. Imagine that. She expected me to find time to hunt for the books she was recommending, to actually read them, and then come back to her office the next week prepared to discuss or complete pages of workbook exercises. I resisted. I balked. I told her I'd never find the time. But she insisted that it was essential, part of the commitment I needed to make to my health and my own needs.

The one assignment that still stands out in my mind all these years later was simple. Or so I thought. It had nothing to do with reading books or answering questions about my past.

"Find one hour for yourself this weekend," Pat instructed at one of our sessions. "One hour. Sixty minutes."

"Well, I could take my son for a walk to the park."

She wasn't hearing it.

"I could stop by the office and catch up on paperwork."

Not happening.

"Drop your son off with your parents and spend one hour doing something that's not required, not productive, not necessary," she told me. "Something for yourself. Just you. Just because."

As it turned out, I did follow her instructions and drove away from my parents' house with an empty car seat in the back and no plan in mind. None at all. I could go to the bank. I could hear Pat saying no. I could run to CVS and pick up some paper towels. No again. Then what? No idea!

As I recall, I stopped for coffee and spent the hour driving around with the radio blasting and no particular destination in mind. But that one hour of driving past the rolling farmlands and sandy beaches where I grew up was good for the spirit that had been fading fast from my life. In the juggling act of raising a child, building a business, and tending to a home, I had dropped the ball. I had neglected the one person on whom everything else depended, around whom everything else revolved.

Never again.

The Mother-Daughter Connection

After a long week and a way-too-long winter, Friday finds me looking forward to a sunny April weekend. Ernie needs to work, so I might catch up on some projects around the house or maybe just kick off and visit a friend, run some errands, or get in a little shopping. That's the plan. Until the phone rings.

"*Mommm.*"

"Hey there, Meredith. How's it going?"

It's a good thing we've got unlimited cell phone minutes between family members. Ever since Meredith left for college, we've been logging hours and hours on the phone, maintaining the connection to home she has needed to carry her through the transition from small town to big city, from living at home to making it on her own, from depending on her parents to relying on herself.

"What are you doing?" I ask.

"Nothing."

I never know what to expect when she calls, but I always get a reading on her very quickly. If there's a squeal in her voice, a high-pitched hello, then she's in a good mood, just checking in, spilling the details of her classes, her friends, her errands, her dancing, even what she had for dinner last night. If she's a bit quieter than that, she's tired. I can tell this from the long lapses in conversation while she

makes her lunch or puts away her laundry; the link to home somehow a comfort as she goes about her daily chores.

"It's almost the weekend! The weather's finally getting nicer!" I say.
"Yep."

There have been some hysterical calls. Something happens, and
she needs help. She loses her school ID and can't get back into the
dorm. She slices her finger instead of the cheese. An explosion goes
off in the middle of the night on the street right below her window.
She can't move her neck on one side from a dance injury. Her debit
card doesn't work for some odd reason. Most of these times, there's
no tangible advice I can offer. All I've got to give is the moral support
of making her feel she isn't alone. Although, truth to tell, she is.

"You've got dance class tomorrow, right?" I ask.
"Yep."

And then there are the other calls. The dark times when her anxiety spikes, the panic in her voice rises, and she feels overwhelmed
by whatever trouble of the day is coming at her. Too much homework. Too much noise from her roommates. A ruffled feeling from
a friend. A dating disaster. The inevitable ups and downs of her first
serious relationship. These calls are difficult. Especially from a distance. There's no eye contact. There's no chance to hug her, or hold
her, or make her a cup of tea. There's no way I can get Lizzie to come
over and kiss her face or curl up at her feet or coax her out for a walk.
All I've got to work with is my voice on the phone, my words strung
together, some unexpected pearl of wisdom that hopefully comes
along at just the right moment.

"How's your friend Chase?"

No response. She's gone dark.

"Meredith, are you there?"

In the end, I'm learning that often, it's not what I say that helps.

It's what I hear. Just taking the time to listen, one human being to another, letting her know her thoughts, feelings, and frustrations fall on empathetic ears. Sometimes, that's all I can do. Listen and soothe her as best as I can, hopefully, hear her stumble on a thought or an idea that will turn her head around. Or her heart. Sometimes I succeed and feel great about my phone mothering, as I like to call it. Other times, like this one, I don't.

"Say something, sweetie!"

I get it. The winter has been long, and the semester, even longer. I think she's had enough about now. Enough of school. Enough of homework. Enough of honking cars and jostling crowds. Enough of running errands in the rain. Enough is enough.

"I've got to go," she says slowly, her voice seeming to spiral lower with each word.

"Don't you want to talk?"

"There's nothing to talk about." Her words trail off in the distance, and then she hangs up. I'm left sitting here with bits and pieces of a dark, disjointed conversation ringing in my ears.

I get up to empty the dishwasher and then take out the trash, but no matter what I do, I can't shake the unsettled feeling in the pit of my stomach. Something about this conversation was different. I call my sister. Denise's idea? Have Meredith come home for the weekend. I think about it. But the disruption to her homework, her dance classes, her friendships, and her routine doesn't seem like it would be good for her right now.

Saturday morning dawns, and while I'm out on my run, all the thoughts of the previous day whirling around in my brain, an idea comes to me, a variation on the theme Denise had suggested. Ernie is working all day, and my projects can wait. So can any errands or shopping. I pick up the phone.

"Hey, Meredith. What are you doing tonight?" I hold my breath as I wait for her to answer.

"Nothing. Why?"

"Because I've got a plan."

"What is it?" She seems a little better this morning. And I've definitely piqued her curiosity.

"I'm hopping on the train in a little while, and I'll be in New York after your dance class. Why don't you pack some things and meet me at the hotel around five o'clock. We'll get dinner and have a sleepover!"

"Really?" For the first time, I detect a hint of enthusiasm in her voice.

"Yes!"

I scurry around the house, making reservations and packing, and finally settle down once I'm on the train. Nestled in a window seat for the three-hour journey to Manhattan, I'm reminded of another ride, another city, another child who needed a lift.

The drive from Jamestown to Washington, DC, was one of the longest I'd ever made alone, but Ernie's work and our family's schedules elected me to pick Geoff up from college his freshman year to bring him home for the summer. I was excited at the prospect of the solo journey and had anticipated arriving at Geoff's dorm to find him all packed and ready to make it home to Rhode Island in time for dinner. When I knocked on his door in the middle of a sunny May morning, I wasn't prepared for what I found.

"It's unlocked," said a voice that sounded like Geoff's, although it was so low and muffled I couldn't be sure.

I pushed the door open and peered inside to find my six-foot-six son curled up on the floor, half asleep amid a jumble of books and notebooks with yellow legal sheets crumpled up into balls all around. "I didn't finish my paper. I haven't even begun packing."

The schedule in my head disappeared. I said, "Isn't there a Starbucks down the hill?"

Between sips of caramel macchiato and bites of spinach feta egg wrap, Geoff began to sit up a little straighter. "I wonder if I could email the paper to my professor from home."

We took our time but managed to get all his stuff packed up and into the car sometime after noon. He helped me navigate the labyrinth of loops on the highway getting out of DC, but our plan to take turns driving was out the window, the same one his head was resting on, although not too comfortably. Gradually, his sentences slowed and then slurred into silence punctuated only by an occasional snore. His deep sleep transported him all nine hours from a semester of exams and papers, lectures and deadlines to a summer of working at the barista job he loved, brushing up on his tennis game, and hanging out with friends.

∽

"Arriving at Penn Station in five minutes!"

The conductor's loud voice and the rumble of the train on the tracks jolt me back to New York. I meet my grown-up girl in the hotel lobby. We head out and get takeout bowls of soup, salad, and our favorite dessert: frozen yogurt. Back at the hotel, we sprawl out on the king-sized bed with our picnic dinner and catch up on things. One-on-one. Face-to-face. Mother-and-daughter.

We chat and eat, and chat and drink, and chat and laugh, and chat some more until, eventually, a wave of tired contentment washes over us. I tuck her into bed with a hug and a kiss. She sleeps better than she has in a long while. I do, too.

Sometimes, when the connection on the phone isn't working, a mother's got to do what we mothers always do. We follow our instincts. We come to the rescue. We show up for our kids, whether that means a trip to New York City or Washington, DC, or any other destination along the way. We don't dither. We don't debate. At a moment's notice, our mothering hat goes on, and we spring into action. Empty nest or not, it always fits us just right.

Stay. Why Don't You Stay?

The two-mile drive from our home on the north end of the island to the center of our little town was long enough. Even the short distance after turning onto the main street and passing the three churches, the fire station, the seafood restaurant, and the pizza place before arriving at the vet's office seemed long. But the ride home with our soon-to-be-seventeen-year-old black Labrador whimpering in the back seat seems infinitely longer.

We had taken Lizzie to get help for what we thought was a urinary infection, her sudden loss of bladder control creating a sense of urgency for us all. We had taken her to get help, perhaps a pill or a shot that would cure whatever was ailing her. But suddenly, Ernie and I are the ones who need help.

Out of the corner of my eye, I catch a glimpse of the man I love tightly gripping the steering wheel, staring straight down the road ahead. I want to say something. I think we should talk. But the vet has already said enough.

How did we get here? How did the routine wellness exams and the visits for an occasional limp or a scrape on the nose give way to the doctor's stern look at our dog and then at us, a pause to adjust his glasses, and then this: "Does Lizzie wake up every morning eager to take on the day?"

The four legs that once bounded over stone walls and leaped up stairs three at a time are now uncertain at best and frequently give out altogether, causing her to slip and slide on our wooden floors until she ultimately gets stuck and panics, unable to move at all. The soft black nose that used to detect a biscuit tucked in my jacket pocket in the hallway closet is now most often found burrowed deep in the nest of blankets we have fashioned for her on the family room floor: she just lies there, day after day after day. The ravenous appetite that once scarfed down breakfast and dinner in record time, the rest of the day spent searching for any snacking opportunities, now seems to have vanished, the food in her bowl going untouched, often for hours.

"You've been lucky," said the vet. "Seventeen years is a long run."

He's right, of course. We're fortunate Lizzie has been happy and healthy all this time, plenty long enough to have inextricably woven her little doggie heart into our family's story. Like the day the banana bread cooling on the kitchen counter mysteriously disappeared, a few crumbs on the floor and a smug look on her face our only clues as to what had happened. Or the time her collar got snagged in the dishwasher rack, and she dragged the whole thing, dishes and all, around behind her, plates and cups clattering and shattering as she raced all over the house trying to break free. Then there were the quieter moments, like naps curled up beside the kids on the rug in the sunny living room. And the times she'd find me sitting for a brief moment at the kitchen table to sew pointe shoes or make a shopping list or text a friend, and she'd wrap her paws around my ankle in a hug as if to say, "Stay. Why don't you stay?"

Now, I'm the one saying that.

How did seventeen years fly by, seventeen years during which a puppy grows into a dog into a family member who fits together with us so perfectly? Why does change force us to let go, leaving us to face the inevitable void, making the emptiness we already feel even emptier?

The truth is, Lizzie is leaving us. Slowly, she's losing ground. Quietly, she's slipping away.

"Chances are, she will not pass in her sleep," said our vet. "This will not be a natural transition, as much as we all wish that for her. That's not the way it typically goes," he said. "Maybe for one dog in a hundred. But those are long odds." He suggested this might be the time for us to act. He wanted us to go home and think. He wanted us to go home and talk.

We are going home. We're driving there with our soon-to-be-seventeen-year-old black Labrador whimpering in the back seat. We're rumbling past the creek and the seafood shack, past the row of towering pine trees and the reservoir just like we have a million times before. But the road doesn't seem so familiar now. Nothing does. Thankfully, the silence between Ernie and me has lifted. We're talking now. We're talking about our beloved dog. How she might be feeling. Why she might be whimpering. What we can do to make her more comfortable.

But when it comes to the particular topic our vet has suggested, we just can't find the words.

The Pink Fairies

It's springtime, and the fairies are back. They're floating on the breeze near the cherry blossom tree at just the right angle so we can see them through the living room picture window. Mom waves her arms at the spectacle from her perch on the blue couch across from the blue chair in the house where I grew up. This is the same house that had been painted red for as long as I could remember until recently when the shingles were replaced by aluminum siding. Dad asked Mom to pick the color. It's blue.

"What's all that outside the window?" Mom asks. "What are those?"

"Fairies!" That's what I tell her. "In pink hats and fancy dresses."

She leans forward on the edge of the couch to get a better look.

"Watch carefully. Every so often, they glide to earth."

"Really?" she asks.

"Yes! And if you're lucky enough to see them and fast enough to catch one, she'll grant you a wish."

This is the same story, more or less, that I told Meredith when she was two or three. But my mother is in her eighties. And yet the enchantment is much the same.

The delight continues when we read *The Secret Garden*. Sometimes we don't even make it through a chapter before her eyes grow heavy and her head bobs to one side or the other. But today, she's sitting up straight and alert, her eyes riveted on me as I turn the pages.

"What's Mary Lennox going to do now?" Mom asks. "What's it like living in that great big house in England?" Her enthusiasm for the tale set on the Yorkshire moors never seems to fade. I wonder if I was as good of a listener all those times when she read it to me.

Mom keeps asking about Mary Lennox, and I keep reading about Mary Lennox. But my mind keeps wandering to another life, another time. Page after page, I'm thinking of Elaine Mary Lussier, the mother who raised me, the navy wife who fearlessly crisscrossed the country as Dad served in three wars, setting up one home after another, finding schools for us, meeting neighbors, and making friends wherever we went. I see it all so clearly. The Girl Scout leader prodding us girls up a rocky trail. The after-school cookie baker greeting us with warm sweetness after a difficult day. The bookkeeper heading back to work to help make our family's budget numbers add up. The ballroom dancer glamorous and glowing in Dad's arms. There she is. The gardener sporting a big straw hat as she tends to the zucchini, radishes, and tomatoes she carefully planted in the backyard. The patient Nana showing her grandkids what magic—not to speak of mess—they can make from flour, sugar, and cinnamon. The student earning her college degree, one night course at a time, just because she loved to learn. No matter how busy she was, she managed to pull it all off with remarkable grace and poise, an understated elegance evident in everything she did.

"Rita! Are you okay?" Mom shifts back and forth on the couch. I must have stopped reading.

Have you ever unexpectedly come into a moment when a knowing wells up inside, and you suddenly realize you'd better hold on to this time? Slow it down. Freeze the frame. Tuck it safely away where you keep your most cherished memories. In that moment, everything feels so right—you know you belong there together, and you just want to savor the closeness for as long as you possibly can.

I set the book down, get up, and wrap my sweater around my shoulders. "I'll be right back," I say as I head out the front door into the soft breeze, which blows pink all around the blue house. I hold my hands in the air and wait. Here she comes now for a landing.

"Look what I caught!" I say as I come back in to show the pink treasure to my mother. "We can make a wish!"

She claps her hands and closes her eyes tightly. Then she takes a deep breath.

It's my turn now. But my wish has already come true. I caught a fairy! She was floating on the breeze near the cherry blossom tree at just the right angle so that the dark clouds couldn't come into view. All Mom and I could see was pink snow, flitting and fluttering, painting a rosy lens on our picture window, at least for the moment. At least for today.

The Move

If only I could get Ricardo to answer his phone, things would turn out all right." I punch the numbers into my cell phone again, checking each digit carefully against the ones scrawled on the crumpled paper I take from my purse.

"You better hope," says Ernie with a sideways glance from his perch in the driver's seat. It's a little before 9:00 on Sunday morning, and we're barreling down a relatively deserted Route 95 toward New York City with a lot on the line.

Without much warning, things have become way too stressful around here. Last night, during a graduation party for my cousin's daughter, when I wanted nothing more than to just kick back and enjoy the evening, my cell phone kept buzzing with other plans. The first message was from Meredith, who had spent the day repainting the walls of the bedroom in her apartment from lavender back to white. That was before she even began to pack. She was wondering what the plan is for moving to her new place. I hated to admit it, but I was wondering, too. The next three or four messages were from Denise with an increasingly frantic report from our parents' house, where things weren't going well with Mom, and Dad was exhausted and running on fumes. Then, one of my friends chimed in with an unusual request for a call back on a weekend due to a squabble with her husband that somehow got out of hand. All these calls coming in on a perfect Saturday evening in June. Well, the weather was perfect anyway.

"I can't believe we came up with this plan so quickly," I say to Ernie as we cross over the line into Connecticut. "It's amazing how fast things come together when they have to."

"Except for one thing. Ricardo! Remember?" says Ernie. "Did he pick up the phone?"

"Listen. I know we should have figured this all out days ago. But so far this morning, we've managed to get our neighbor to watch Lizzie, we've booked a hotel room for tonight, and we've got movers coming tomorrow to pick up all the stuff in Meredith's old apartment and transport it to her new one."

"That's all great. Amazing, actually. But he's not answering his phone!"

"Maybe he's busy painting and cleaning and moving junk out of the apartment he's subletting to us. Yes, that must be why he's not answering. He's too busy getting ready. That has to be it."

Then, somewhere deep into Connecticut, Ernie's concern growing by the mile, we finally make contact. Ricardo assures me he's working on the apartment. Getting it all ready. And he'll meet us outside the building at 10:00 tomorrow morning with the key. Yay! With her roommate moving and the lease on their old apartment about to expire, Meredith was excited to find a studio on a tree-lined street in Chelsea that came up for subletting. Like everything else in New York City, things happen fast. Hopefully, the move will, too.

Outside what will be her new apartment building on Sixteenth Street, Meredith and I arrive on time the next morning, eager to get the ball rolling. The plan is to get the key from Ricardo, go up to the third floor, and take a look at her new, clean, and freshly painted place, then head over to her old apartment to wait for the movers. We've just got to get the key.

"Is that Ricardo? The guy with the dog coming toward us?" I ask Meredith, although she couldn't possibly know the answer. "There was an animal cage in the apartment when we had looked at it with the realtor several weeks ago. Maybe that's him and his dog." Guess not. He walks right past us.

"Could that be him? The guy in the business suit?" I ask.

"How about the one on the skateboard?" Meredith says. "Or the man with the backpack crossing the street? Or maybe the guy with the headphones?"

As amusing as our little guessing game is, time is ticking by. We've got a lot to do. Whoever Ricardo is, wherever he is, he's late. Fifteen minutes, to be exact. Good thing Ernie stayed back at the hotel to work instead of sweating it out here on the sidewalk with Meredith and me. He hates to be late and despises it even more if there's any inconvenience involved. Like now.

Okay. It's 10:30. Time for action. Time to call the realtor. No, she hasn't heard from Ricardo. She has no idea where he is or what's going on.

At this point, I leave Meredith waiting on the sidewalk in the dwindling hope that Ricardo will show up while I take matters into my own hands. I sneak inside the front door of the apartment building behind a tenant and take the elevator to the third floor to see for myself what's going on. Maybe I can get in. The apartment door wasn't locked the other day when we came with the realtor. And look at that! It isn't locked today. And look at this! A peek inside confirms my worst fears. No one has been here. Nothing has happened. The paint is still peeling off the walls. The dust is still gathering on the floors. The streaks are still muddying up the windows. And the stinky dog cage is still sitting here, smack in the middle of the floor. Yikes!

This is one of those days when the stars are out of alignment. My sister would say Mercury is in retrograde. Whatever the interplanetary explanation, what I've come to learn during these times, often the hard way, is that here on earth, nothing is going to go smoothly. Whatever balls you're juggling will fall to the ground. Meteors are likely to come crashing at you out of the blue. And all you can do is hang on tight, make the best of the situation, and come out the other side.

Back on the sidewalk with Meredith, I do the only thing I can think of. Cancel the movers. The guy is not happy. He spews some not-very-nice words into the phone. I can't blame him. Those same words might have crossed my mind when I walked into the dingy apartment and thought of my phone conversation with Ricardo just yesterday while Ernie and I were driving down Route 95 on our way to New York. But fortunately, those words haven't slipped out of my lips. Not yet.

Since Ernie can't leave the city until later in the day, after work, Meredith and I spend the rest of our time searching for a silver lining in this upsetting turn of events. We find two. While we're hanging out at her old apartment, we learn that her roommate is planning on giving away her oversized couch since it won't work in her new place. But it will look nice and fit perfectly in Meredith's, so we take it! And then I go back and forth on the phone negotiating with the realtor who claims that Ricardo *promises* to have the place ready later in the week. And to make up for our inconvenience, he's offering to pay one month's rent.

So, let's see. We get one free couch and one free month's rent. We'll take it!

We sure have a lot to tell Ernie on our long ride home, which turns out to be a good thing because our car overheats, and we learn from a gas station mechanic somewhere in Connecticut that there's something wrong with the thermostat. So we end up driving in the slow lane, keeping the speed under forty-five miles per hour, with the heat on full blast like a sauna to somehow stabilize the control until we can get it fixed, the sweat pouring off us along with our frustration.

What else can possibly go wrong?

Try, Try Again

If at first you don't succeed at moving, board a train and head to New York City. Again. Second trip in a week. Surely, things will go as planned this time. Ricardo will show up with the keys. The apartment will be clean and neat, freshly scrubbed and painted. The move will come off as scheduled. Even if it is three days later than we had intended.

"I really should be home planning the Fourth of July party for tomorrow," I say to Meredith as we settle into our seats, and the train rumbles away from the station. "I should be looking up recipes. Shopping at the market. Making the new potato salad."

"It's okay, Mom. We'll get it done. I'll help with everything tomorrow."

"Odd thing about the potato salad. Your nana got so excited when I read the recipe to her. These days, she doesn't seem to show much emotion about anything. But she said she couldn't wait to try it."

"We'll make a great potato salad tomorrow," Meredith says. "It'll be delicious."

I take a deep breath and look out the window at the haze hanging over the seacoast in the distance.

New York welcomes us with sweltering heat and humidity. Dark clouds gather in the northern sky. We hurry to the apartment building. When we get there, the realtor is outside waiting for us, keys in her hand. Upstairs, on the third floor, we're delighted to find Meredith's new place painted and cleaned. We spend an hour or so tidying up, measuring windows and walls, and making a list of cleaning supplies we're going to need. A big project, to be sure. But this time, at least, we get the chance to begin. We lock and bolt the door and walk a mile or so over to her old apartment to pack up several last-minute items and wait for the movers. What a difference a few days make!

As it turns out, there's not much to do here but wait. "I think I'll pack up this handcart with some of my more delicate things," Meredith says, gathering a few of her treasures and setting them on the coffee table. "My jewelry, vases, glasses, this earring tree. I can walk them over to my new apartment and be back before the movers come."

"Okay. I'll wait here in case they show up early."

As I sit here alone in the sudden solitude amid all the boxes, I'm grateful for a break in the action. Just me and my thoughts. Until my phone rings.

"Mommy!" She never calls me that. "I lost the keys!"

The keys? Please be the old keys. Please be the old keys. Please be the old keys. That would be no problem. I'm already here at the old apartment, so I don't need the old keys. And if I did, I have a spare set conveniently tucked right here in my purse.

I wait for her reply, although somewhere in the pit of my stomach, I already know what I'm going to hear. That planets-out-of-alignment thing must still be happening. Brace yourself. "The new keys!" Meredith says. "I lost the new keys to my new place!"

Never mind how it happened, how you thought they were in your hands or in the cart. No time for that now. "Just stay calm," I tell her on the phone, trying to do the same myself. "Turn around. Go back the exact same way you came. Look everywhere along your path for the missing keys that are hopefully still there somewhere in the road or on the sidewalk."

They are not. She's back here in the old apartment with me now. We have no keys and no plan.

I do the only thing I can think of under the circumstances. I put Meredith in charge of the old apartment and the movers, and I head out into the sweltering day. I have no clue where I'm going, what I'm going to do, or how I'm going to fix this problem: the movers packing up everything at the old apartment only to arrive at the new one, their truck loaded to the hilt, with no way to get in. Instinctively, I switch into that gear we mothers seem to possess when we get into these kinds of situations with our kids. We have no idea how we're going to solve what's confronting us except for one. We will solve it.

Slowly, carefully, I retrace my daughter's path on the sidewalks and in the streets. No shining objects to be found. No keys. No luck.

I call the realtor, hoping she's got an extra set that she forgot to give us. No answer. I call Ricardo, hoping his lack of attention to detail might work in our favor this time around, and he might have inadvertently hung onto a spare. No answer. I leave messages for both of them and move on to the next thing. Whatever that is.

Before long, I'm waiting outside the new apartment building. A young woman with shopping bags lets herself into the lobby, and I follow behind. I take the elevator to the third floor and try the door to Meredith's apartment, hoping against hope that it's not locked and bolted. But, of course, it is. We left it that way.

I call the superintendent, Jose, and hope that he will answer my call and possibly even my prayers. He shows up with his toolbox and a sense of shared purpose even though we just met this very minute. I glance at my phone. Two thirty, it says. One hour or so before the movers show up.

I stand there awkwardly in the hallway behind Jose, watching as he tries screwdrivers and wrenches and long, skinny wires to no avail. He asks me why we bolted the door in the first place. A good question to which, of course, I have no good answer.

"I'm going to my office," he says. "I'll be right back."

Minutes later, he comes back with an entire pocket full of keys. He tries each of them, one after another. None of them fits. None of them works. Ricardo must have changed the lock and never given the new key to Jose. No surprise there.

In our mission to break into my daughter's new apartment, I've got two jobs. The first is to hold a flashlight steady on the door so Jose can see what he's doing in the dark hallway. The second is to stay in touch with Meredith at her old apartment. I'm hoping, of course, not to hear what we're not yet ready to hear: that the movers have arrived at her old place, that they've packed everything up, and they're heading our way.

A look at the sweat dampening the back of Jose's blue work shirt tells me one thing I already know and another that I'm quickly learning. One, it's damn hot in this hallway. Two, this is no ordinary superintendent. He's kneeling on the wooden floor, bent down over his toolbox, pulling out one device and then another with a level of intensity and persistence you'd expect to see if this were his own daughter. Each tool produces the same result: no result. If only we hadn't bolted the door. If only we hadn't lost the key. If only Ricardo had done what he said he was going to do several days ago, we would not be standing here on this sweltering eve of the Fourth of July. But here we are.

The latest text from Meredith buzzes on my phone. The movers have packed everything up back at the old apartment and they're leaving! They're on their way! My phone says it's 3:30 p.m. How long can it take them to go five blocks?

Jose is on to a small drill. Metal chips fly in the heavy air. My hand stiffens from holding the flashlight. Jose's shirt is drenched, sticking to his back like my tank top after a long run. I could use a long run now. Very long.

He takes out a bigger drill. The sound reverberates throughout the quiet hallway, where I imagine the residents are long gone, already having made their escape from the city on their way to holiday weekends in relaxing destinations. Seashores with ocean breezes. Beach cottages with air-conditioned verandas. Poolside loungers with piña coladas. Cool things. Lovely things. Summertime things.

Chunks of metal and wood fill the air as the clock on my phone flips to 4:00, and then, finally, it happens. The door gives way. Sunlight floods into the hallway from the windows in Meredith's apartment. Jose did it! We're in! And not a minute too soon. The movers have arrived.

Somewhere between burly men bustling in and out of the door, Meredith holes up in the galley kitchen, talking with her boyfriend on the phone. An argument of some sort is brewing, I suspect. It's hard to tell for sure in the midst of all the coming and the going, the commotion of men and furniture and boxes moving all around.

As Jose drills off the shards of lock that hang from the door, it suddenly hits me. We now have a bigger problem than we had unlocking the door. Locking it! It's after 5:00 p.m. on the day before the Fourth of July weekend in New York City, and the entire population seems to be heading out of town. How are we going to get a locksmith here to close it back up? Disturbing images swarm my brain of Meredith and me spending the next three days in her apartment, the lockless apartment, instead of taking the train home.

As luck would have it—and I do mean good luck this time, make that unbelievable, amazingly great luck!—Jose calls a locksmith friend, who just happens to be in the area and, despite the holiday weekend that's upon us, just happens to be willing to get the job done. And he does. Just in time for Meredith and me to catch our train. But, of course, not before angry white zigzags of lightning bisect the blackening skies, crackling here and there on the sidewalks all around us, the holiday eve commute transformed into a mad dash for shelter.

Before we reach Penn Station, we're completely and utterly soaked. Not unexpectedly, Meredith melts down as soon as the train begins rolling away, her tender contents having come under pressure for far too long, the unsettling events of the day and the week preventing her from getting settled and relaxing on our three-hour journey home.

"It's okay. Try to get some rest, sweetie," I say and pat her gently on the knee, arranging the sweatshirt over her shoulders like a blanket. "Everything will be okay."

That's what I tell her.

That's what I tell myself.

The Fourth of July

"It's not going to rain," Ernie says before I set out on my six-mile run. We've driven over the bridge to Newport with a plan to meet at our favorite coffee shop for breakfast in an hour. I glance at the dark clouds gathering to the west and tell myself not to worry. He checks the weather on his phone, and the nearest rain is three states away. I'll be fine. I'm also reassured by all the other early risers out here with me in the dawning hours of the holiday, getting their runs, walks, and bike rides in before their barbecues and picnics. The streets and sidewalks of this charming city bustle with an unusual amount of activity for such an early hour. No rain today, they all assure me.

Halfway through my run, about as far from the coffee shop as I'm going to get—or any shelter, for that matter—the clouds burst open. The storm has followed me home from New York. The rain is unrelenting. The thunder and lightning no less so. There's no getting around it, no dodging the bullet, no running for cover. I'm caught smack in the middle of the road with no place to hide. Within seconds, I'm drenched from head to toe, as soaked as Lizzie is after retrieving a stick at the seashore.

"Would you rather go home and dry off?" Ernie asks as I take my perch next to him at the coffee shop, having slogged my way there in the rain. Shivering on a stool, I look out the window at the torrents of

130

water falling on Washington Square that are sure to cancel the patriotic concert and reading of the Declaration of Independence outside the Colony House later this morning. "We can pack this stuff up and make a run for the car."

"Let's sit for a while," I say, warming my hands on the cup of coffee Ernie had waiting for me. I look over at him as he takes a bite of his egg sandwich. "I'm just happy to be here with you."

After catching my breath for a few moments, I fill him in on the events in New York the day before, sharing the details of our second attempt at moving Meredith into her new apartment. "Throwing together a last-minute Fourth of July bash for the family will be a piece of cake compared to what went on in Manhattan yesterday." That's what I tell him. That's what I think.

But then we get back into the car, and I check my phone. Even before I listen to the voicemails from my sister, all five of them, I know. Something is wrong.

We race home, where I shower, pack a few things, and head over to my parents' house. Through the picture window in the living room, I see Mom and Dad. Despite the pelting rain and booming thunder, they are fast asleep.

What I discover in the den as I peer into the window near the back door is not much more encouraging. Denise sits cross-legged on the couch, her hands outstretched, her eyes closed in a meditative pose.

I let myself in through the garage. My sister tells me that while I was in New York, it's been a rough couple of days back home. "Mom isn't doing well. She isn't eating anything or drinking much or sleeping well. She's growing increasingly uncomfortable and more and more agitated."

"Hi Dad," I say as I see my father come into the room. His face is drawn and drained, just like my sister's. They are looking to me for something. Energy. Inspiration. Something.

"Your Mom isn't doing well," he says. "We need to do something."

"Would it help if we stayed here with you to care for her?" I ask. "Or if we took turns?"

Dad shakes his head and stares down at the rug. "She needs professional care. We can't give her what she needs. Not anymore."

"What if we got a home health care service to stay here?" Denise asks.

"I don't know. I just don't know."

After a long discussion, we decide the best plan is to drive Mom to the emergency room, hope that she's admitted overnight, and then go from there to wherever the doctors lead us: assisted living, home health care, a nursing home, or a psychiatric evaluation facility. Clearly, things cannot continue as they have around here for the last four years, Dad caring for her every need with so much love and affection yet wearing down with every day that passes. It's not that he can't keep going. He has more energy than any other man I know. But it's time. She needs specialized care and round-the-clock attention. And we need help. We all agree on that.

Resigned, Dad gets up and stands in the doorway. He looks at us, his two girls. "Elaine is a good woman. A good wife. A good mother. And if she can't stay home any longer, if God wants her," he says, "I won't stand in the way."

The wind howls outside the window, the dark storms gathering strength on this summer holiday, both outside and in. We manage to get Mom to sit up on the couch. We pull on her sweater and slip on her jacket, but before we get her up off the couch, Dad pauses and finds the blue comb on the table. He runs it through her hair. He leans over to give her a kiss. "There, now, dear. Beautiful. You are beautiful!"

Perhaps, I think, we never realized just how strong and determined our mother really is, just how much faith she has in God, until these last four years when Alzheimer's began stealing her away. She has never complained. On the contrary, even when she has struggled to speak, she has somehow found words to ask how we're doing, always offering us encouragement, and still taking the time to express her affection for us.

In the ultimate act of love, my father has been right here by her side every step of the way. As she has gotten weaker, he has grown stronger. The more she forgets, the more he has remembered. As she has withdrawn from the world, he has reached out, finding new ways to care and compensate. His enduring love and faith have kept her home, safe and sound, for these last four years until now, until this stormy holiday, this Fourth of July.

There's something surreal about these moments as we get Mom ready to go. How Dad takes the time to comb her hair before we leave. How tenderly he speaks to her as he fastens the straps of her rain bonnet beneath her chin. And then there's the long walk with Mom out of the house. Denise on one side. Me on the other. Step by step, slowly, oh so slowly, walking out of the living room, through the kitchen, down the hallway, across the den, until finally Mom's legs buckle under her, and her entire body goes limp in our arms at the threshold of the garage. She refuses to walk, refuses to budge. And she doesn't. We can only manage to hold her there awkwardly in a semi-upright position near the cold, damp garage and dial 911.

Denise rides along in the ambulance. Dad and I take separate cars to the hospital. We end up spending the Fourth of July in the emergency room where Mom gets tested, rehydrated, and eventually moved to the second floor to stay overnight.

When I finally leave the hospital sometime later that evening, the skies are still threatening, the wind still gusting, the rain pelting down all around me. I don't see or hear or feel any of it. All I can do is sit in the blackness of my car, clutching my keys and holding my breath.

When we're swallowed by the darkness, the road ahead is invisible.

The Eighth of July

It's early morning, and I'm out running in the sultry air, all alone on the road. No cars. No bikes. No walkers. No dogs on leashes. Just me. Running past impossibly green lawns and fanciful gardens. Past shimmering waters and rocky beaches. Past tidy houses, the children inside still nestled in their beds, another carefree day of summer vacation awaiting them. July is perfect right now. There's not a cloud in the sky, and not a care in the world. Except in mine. There are cares. There are most definitely cares. I will not be able to run past them like I often do. Not today. The best I can manage is to divide their weight into little pieces, tiny tasks that I can face one at a time.

Take a shower. Get dressed in something cheerful. Maybe my pink dress? Leave early enough to pick up two coffees and a tea and bring them to the hospital to buoy Dad, Denise, and myself for the 10:00 a.m. meeting with the doctor. Get ready to discuss the inevitable nursing home option, though I hate the thought of it. Be open to considering the psychological evaluation Denise suggested a week or so ago. Don't forget to ask about the potato salad. How is it possible that just last week Mom was sitting on the couch with me helping to plan the menu for our Fourth of July party? How can she go from there, encouraging me to try a new recipe for her favorite summer dish, to here, lying limp and listless in a hospital bed? Ask these questions, ask more questions, ask all the questions at the meeting at the hospital. Find out what's best for her. I'm ready. I'm ready for anything.

Anything except for the call on my cell in my car on the way to the hospital before the stop for coffee. Denise's voice is shaken but somehow steady. "I got to the hospital early. I'm here. Rita. Mom is gone."

Mom is gone? Denise's mom is gone. But my mother? My mother is gone. Gone?

I drive to the hospital. Where I'm heading, I have no idea. My thoughts are disconnected, disjointed. My vision is clogged, cloudy. I try focusing. I try concentrating on taking it slowly.

One. Step. At. A. Time.

Park the car. Take the keys. Lock the door. Walk steady. Act like I know what I'm doing. Look like I know where I'm going. I see my father heading up to the front door of the hospital, his gait unmistakable, still brisk from all his years as bandmaster in the navy. I could never keep up with him then. Now I have no choice. Oh God. I have to catch him. I have to tell him. Why is this happening? Why now? I can't let him go up the elevator and down the hallway, saying "hello" to this nurse and "how are you" to that patient, only to find the love of his life, his precious wife, in the room at the end of the hall and learn that she is there, but she is not.

How do you tell your father that the woman he has been married to for sixty-three years and loved for even longer is gone, somehow having slipped away from us in the night when we weren't looking? She would have wanted it that way. Is that what you tell him? She did want it that way! She wanted to spare us, I'm sure. She's always looking out for us. Oh God. Who's going to look out for us now? My sister will be brokenhearted. And Dad, I just don't know what he'll do, how he'll go on.

Then there's my aunt in California, my mother's only sister. My kids, who are so close to their nana. Who will look out for us now? Who will care for, nurture, and guide us? Who will be there to remind us of peace and love and beauty when we get lost? And we do get lost.

I catch up to Dad. I say words I can't comprehend. We go up to the room. We see Mom there, but not really. A nurse comes into the room. She says something to comfort us, but it doesn't. Her words can't cut through the fog in my brain. A doctor comes in. He's talking, too. I hear him, but it's as if he's speaking to us in Italian or German or Pig Latin. Then in comes the priest. He begins praying. He's asking us to join in. We all hold hands. I try following his lead, saying words together with Dad and Denise that I learned when I was the little girl at the altar rail who believed that saying these prayers, repeating them over and over and over again as if in a trance, would make it all better. Make it all better. Make it all better. Please, God. Please.

We're walking out of the hospital and into the parking lot and getting into our cars. We're meeting Dad at the funeral home. I'm driving Denise. We are stopping for coffee. That is my idea, my only one so far today. It's afternoon, and maybe caffeine will help. In front of me, in line at the coffee shop, is my daughter's ballet teacher. I've known Miss Miki since Meredith started dancing at age three. Miki is supposed to be here, I think. She knows I am shaken even if I don't tell her. But I do. I tell her everything though my words make no sense. Miki has been here before. Last winter. She understands. I know this in the way she comforts me without having to say a word. I feel this in the way she hugs me.

As it turns out, there will be many hugs in the days to come. From my husband, who gathers me into his arms when I finally make it home later in the day. From Geoff, who calls on his way from Boston to the hospital that evening when I have to stop him from his intended visit. From Meredith, who takes the train home from New

York. From my best friend, Carol, who texts me every day for weeks and weeks to let me know that she is there if I need her. I do need her! From Morna and Bill, two friends out on their walk the next morning when I almost run past them, then go back to tell them the news. Despite the sweaty tank top clinging to my back, my face a slippery mess, they stand there in the middle of the road, hugging me. From Ted, a perfect stranger in the best sense of the expression who happens to be sitting next to me at Starbucks on Saturday morning when I go there with my laptop to write the eulogy. From our cousins who come out and stay with us at the wake, at the funeral, and even after that, never having to say anything, just comforting us with their prayers, and their presence. From our friends, our neighbors, and my yoga class. All of them there for us with kind words and caring thoughts that, in the days and weeks and months ahead, will begin to ease the emptiness, will help to fill the void.

But not her shoes. We know this all too deeply. Nothing and no one will fill them. Not today. Not tomorrow. No one. Not ever.

A New Rhythm

What's that sound? What's that tapping on the windows? It's not supposed to rain, but no matter. I couldn't care less. Something good is happening here. I'm already up. I'm dressed. I'm grabbing my laptop and gym bag and heading out into the first gray light of morning.

Before the sun rises, I arrive at the gym. I'm not the only one up early. "Hey Jonathon," I say to the manager as I head to the treadmill. I glance over at the guy on the one next to me; he's already worked up a good sweat. "Good morning, Joe. Looks like you've got a head start on me today."

One great perk of a routine is that the miles fly by. Literally. Before I know it, I'm stretching and heading to the locker room with a sense of accomplishment and it's not even 8:00 a.m.

Next stop, the café. I walk up to the counter and say hello but nothing more. Here comes the part I love.

"Good morning, Rita," says Jenna. "Here's your dark roast, steamed milk with a sprinkle of cinnamon." She smiles as she pours my morning ritual into a cup.

I thank her, pull up a big cushioned chair near the window, and settle in. Out of my bag come the books. Stephen King. Madeleine L'Engle. Annie Dillard. Writers who share their insights on writing, on going deep. Then I visit for a chapter or two with authors whom, over the years, I've begun thinking of as friends, literary pals who lift me up with their words and their takes on life. Anna Quindlen. Nora Ephron. Dominique Browning. Others. Then it's time for a ten-minute or so entry into my journal. A glance at my email. And then on to my writing.

My writing!

After all the procrastination, all the excuses, all the fits and starts, I'm finally putting myself first. To be certain, I know I'm needed elsewhere. My husband, my son, my daughter, my dad, my sister, my friends, my dog, the house, the bills, the bookkeeping for Ernie's business, the calls, the laundry, the chores, the errands, all those people, all those things—they're all still waiting for me. But for now, for this moment, I am writing. That's it. That's enough. I'm honoring my commitment to my muse and myself, and I'm letting it go. For the first time in a long while, I feel good. I feel alive, happily aligned with the stars.

Since I've been coming to this café, my writing mojo is back. Something about getting away from it all, not straightening up the house first, not throwing in a load of laundry, none of that. I'm free to write. Free to focus. For a few hours in the morning, this is my work. This is my job. I don't bring my planner. I don't make a long list of things to do. I don't return phone calls or texts unless they're urgent. I just come here, the workout still fresh in my bones, the shower having washed away my sweat and any lingering doubts, and I show up ready to work. I write until I'm done and not a moment earlier.

In my writing, as I lay down word after word, I'm slowly putting the pieces together, seeing how they can fit in a new and amazing way. This word processing is my thought processing, my search for meaning as I hold moment after moment up to the light and try to see my life more clearly.

We all need this centering, this grounding, so that we can truly claim our best selves. We need to write or read or walk or run or talk or meditate or sing or dance or stand on our heads, or come to whatever practice it is that allows us the time and space to try to make sense of it all. To reconcile the ups and downs of our moments and our days. To find our footing so that we can arrive again at that place where we're peaceful and content, where we show up as the best we can be.

Back at home, it's still raining. Lizzie doesn't even crawl out of her bed to greet me when I come in. Not that I blame her. But the dreary day outside can't dampen what I feel inside: gratitude for this moment.

Listen to how peaceful it is here, the dog snoring, the heater whirring, the house creaking and groaning its age. Look at how I can design my days in any way I want, get things done at my own pace, in my own way of doing them, no longer wrapping my schedule around someone else's. I can get up from the computer to straighten a room, or make the bed, check on the laundry, or text a friend, and then I can settle back down, back to work. I can meet Ernie for a walk at lunchtime and then go back to the house knowing that for the entire afternoon, I can do whatever it is I want or need to get done. Isn't it nice to know that at the end of the day, we can fit in a few errands, go out for coffee, take a drive or a long walk or a yoga class? Yes! Whatever I want. Whatever we want.

Recently, there was a hectic moment at the gym during school vacation when the kids from the pool were running this way and that, hollering and shrieking and rollicking through the hallways and the locker rooms. I caught a glimpse of two harried mothers trying to carry on a conversation despite the challenge of their young charges, clinging to the fragile chance to connect with each other, a little mother-to-mother empathy, a moment of adult-to-adult under-standing. I recognized their desperate yearning immediately. Not so long ago, they were me.

But now I am here.

This place, this moment in time, is surely the antidote prescribed for me. After all those years of school buses and parent shuttles, tennis lessons and ballet classes, homework problems and play dates, scheduling conflicts and last-minute plans, I am here.

I miss my kids terribly and completely. I do. But at this point in my life, I love taking care of myself, too, with the tenderness I learned from my mom. A gift I didn't fully appreciate at the time, but I now know was priceless.

Shades of Gray and Yellow

O n this dreary morning after a sunny long weekend, I'm scheduled to meet my friend Sharon in Newport. Why did I agree to this? Didn't I know how tired I'd feel? Didn't I know how much work would be piled up after taking a few days off? What was I thinking? *Was* I even thinking at all?

But here I am at a café ordering coffee and letting it cool while I wait. And here she is, no doubt weary from her weekend escapades but happy to see me nonetheless. She orders a cup of tea, and we opt to walk out in the gray morning. It's cloudy. It's cool. But as I match my stride to hers, I begin to warm up.

"Are you ready for your daughter's wedding?" I ask. "Unbelievable that the little girl who used to tag along with us to the tennis courts is getting married!"

"Have you made any decisions about your house?" She wants to know. "The last time we talked, you were leaning toward renovating."

"How are your parents? Are they coming to visit this summer?"

"What's new with your writing?"

"We've got so much to catch up on! How long has it been since I've seen you?"

We set out at a brisk pace that matches our conversation as we wind our way through Washington Square, past the old movie theater, and the new Lululemon that sells yoga clothes. Then, we head up the hill past the brick courthouse and the historic Touro Synagogue, the first one in the country.

"So, my fireplace blew up!" Sharon says.

"Say what?"

"Some defect caused it to explode, and there was damage to our living room. Now I'm trying to get the fireplace company to pay for not just a new fireplace but also a couch, curtains, everything."

"But no one was hurt?"

"Thankfully."

We turn onto Bellevue Avenue, a long, relatively straight road lined with trees, stone walls, old-fashioned streetlights, and some remarkable stately homes. So many tourists come to Newport to stroll down this elegant road past the grand summer "cottages" of the Gilded Age, and most of the time, I take it for granted. But not today. I'm alive! I'm awake!

"How's the calligraphy going? Are you crazy busy this wedding season?" I ask. Sharon's eyes are so blue, such a striking contrast to the gray haze all around.

"I'm already booked up, which is good after a slow winter. Speaking of which, did you get to go anywhere warm? Florida? I know how much you love the cold."

"Ha! No, we didn't, and no, I don't."

As we stand on the corner waiting for the light to turn, Sharon spies a riot of orange tiger lilies near a stone wall. "How I love this time of year!"

"Geez, this is like all those times in the locker room," I say. "Except we're not just sitting and talking. We've probably logged in three or four miles by now."

"It's strange not playing tennis. I miss seeing you every week." Sharon slows down to take one last sip of her tea.

"Me, too. But this walk is good. And it's definitely more relaxing than our matches. We used to get so intense when we were playing."

"But it was fun. It felt good."

"I know what you mean. Every Friday, we got to focus on one yellow ball. Not two or three kids, a dog, a business, what's for dinner, who did or didn't do their homework, and all the other things coming at us. We just showed up on the court and let everything go."

As we head back down the hill to our cars, which are parked near the café, I'm left to wonder. Wasn't it busier then when we were young mothers, young wives? Why do we tend to feel so harried much of the time that we say "no" all too often? Sure, we might have lots of things on our minds, on our plates, and on our schedules. But are we really so busy that we don't have one hour or so a week just for fun? Aren't there some things that just feel so right that we have to make time for them?

"Hope to see you sooner next time around," Sharon says as she reaches out to give me a hug before climbing into her car.

"Have a good week," I say, standing on the sidewalk as I wave and then watch her driving away.

On this gray morning after a long weekend, after three or four miles of walking and waking up, I'm starting to reconsider. Maybe the more complicated and busy life gets and the more overwhelming my responsibilities seem, the more essential it might be to get back to a once-a-week commitment to focus on nothing but a yellow ball.

And a very dear friend.

The Longest Walk

"My vote was no, so I should be okay."

Despite being alone, I say this loudly over and over and over again as I make my way up the brick walkway that leads to our house. That I had to go back seventeen years to find this reassurance for myself is troubling, back to when the dog was just a wish, albeit a persistent one coming from Meredith. That was when I voted no. Wouldn't you? Life was already complicated, with barely enough time on any given day to catch my breath. Would you choose to make that life more complicated? Would you willingly agree to even more activity and more responsibility, not to speak of the scratches on the furniture and the accidents on the floor?

But as so often happens in families, my will gave way to the majority, the enthusiasm for a pet winning the day and bringing a black Labrador puppy into our lives. Upon her arrival, Lizzie quickly proceeded to make all my predictions—and new ones—come true.

More activity? Oh yes. Lizzie came leaping and bounding into our home, jumping and running, wiggling and squirming and getting into things left and right. Quickly, we had to change our ways to keep up with her. We started walking every day, at least a mile, maybe two, to help channel her energy and boost ours. We became more playful, the kids inventing games like "Ring the Doorbell," which got Lizzie running to the front door while they hid under the pillows on the couch or the blankets on the bed until she sniffed them out, not hard to do with all their giggling. We found ourselves going to the shore to throw sticks for her to fetch out of the ocean, to the path in the woods where she'd uncover treasures like dead mice, and out to romp in the snow no matter how cold the wind might blow.

"My vote was no, so I should be okay."

My mantra gets louder as I step up to the front door, trying to remember my objections from all those years ago.

A pet is more responsibility. That's what I had said, and how true. But what I could never have envisioned was that Lizzie would become the first truly shared responsibility for our family, for all four of us. On some days, I would take her along on my morning run, or if that didn't happen, get her out for a walk and prod the others to join us. Ernie made sure she got her shots and made it to vet visits on time; he was always looking out for her health and safety. Not a day went by that he didn't insist we keep her on her leash, determined not to have something happen to her. The kids were enthusiastic helpers when it came to playing and feeding, and maybe not so enthusiastic when all that food ran its course, although they did manage to get her outside when she needed to get there.

Yes, I'm sure there were the occasional scratches on the furniture and accidents on the floor, but I can't remember them clearly now. What I do recall are the times I would find her napping in the sunlight on the living room rug with one kid or another sleeping by her side. Then there was the way she shook the entire car as she swayed back and forth with uncontrollable excitement whenever we pulled up at our favorite ice cream stand, the promise of the soon-to-come Dog Bone Sundae too much for her to contain her enthusiasm. And the day she refused to walk with me, just plunked her furry self down at the end of the driveway and wouldn't budge. As I stood there coaxing and then scolding, I looked up to see Ernie's car heading toward us. Apparently, Lizzie had heard him coming long before he turned into the neighborhood, and she decided to wait for him to join us on our walk. So many memories. I have to stop.

What I really need to remember is this: The puppy I thought would be a mistake turned out to be a perfect fit for our family. Even for me.

"My vote was no, so I should be okay."

I open the door and walk down the hallway. I hear my footsteps on the wooden floor, my heart pounding in my chest. I see the water in her bowl and the biscuits on the counter. Toys cascade from her basket, and the oversized L. L. Bean bed with Lizzie embroidered on its side sits in the corner of the family room. I stand there in the kitchen, my body motionless, my thoughts scattering here then there. I wait. For what? Something. Anything. But there's no greeting, no wagging, no commotion, no I'm-so-happy-that-you're-home-I-can-hardly-contain-myself romp around the house that never grew old. Even long after she did. There's none of that. All gone. Just empty. Empty.

My vote was no, and God, was I wrong.

And the part about being okay?

Not even close.

Acceptance is a Virtue

Ten minutes or so after it's been decided that he needs to stay in the rehabilitation facility for another two weeks instead of going home as scheduled, my father leaves a long message on my phone. He makes a point of speaking slowly so that I can take notes.

"Reets," he says. "I need you to get some things from my house. My cell phone is in the little cubby in my car. It should be fully charged. But just in case, the charger is in your bedroom." I love that he calls it my bedroom. Even after all these years.

"Also, I need stamps, address labels, and note cards, which you'll find in the drawers of my desk. And don't forget the thumbtacks." He must mean paper clips. Yes, I'm sure he does. "I really appreciate you doing this for me. I don't know what I'd do without you girls."

When I arrive at the rehabilitation facility the next morning, his favorite Dunkin' Donuts coffee in one hand, a bag filled with his requested supplies in the other, I watch him go about the business of setting up shop. There, in the corner of his room, the nightstand has become his filing cabinet. His bedside table is now his desk. The rocker is his chair. And with that, he's ready to go about conducting the daily routine of his life, keeping himself busy, making his days productive, no matter where he is or what circumstances he might find himself in.

Maybe his ability to make do with what he has, to make his home wherever he happens to find himself, was born out of necessity. Growing up the youngest of twenty-one children (not a typo!), he and his brothers and sisters ate dinner in shifts and slept three to a bed. If his childhood didn't teach him enough about how to make the best of what was available, then joining the navy at age eighteen was all the education he needed. He quickly learned to turn a mug of black navy-issue coffee into a morning ritual; to express a genuine interest in other people's lives, total strangers though they might be; and to appreciate beauty, even tucked away in a little sanctuary he made for himself on the deck of a ship while waiting for the sun to rise on an early-morning watch. That is how he made his way in the world from World War II to Korea to Vietnam and all the places in between.

This way of his, this uncanny ability to accept what comes, to adapt and change course at a moment's notice, lies at the core, in my opinion, of why he recently celebrated his ninety-second birthday. It's not as though it's been smooth sailing. It hasn't. In the time since we lost Mom, his wife of sixty-three years, there have been heart ailments, a hip replacement, a broken wrist, a small stroke, a blood infection, and a stubborn gallstone. Yet always, there he was, rising to the occasion, finding a silver lining.

As we've traveled through these challenges together, he's said to me many times, "I am where I am. I don't know why. I'm not sure what's coming at me next. But I'm grateful to be here, with all the love and care that surrounds me. Might as well make the best of it."

Might as well make the best of it.

His words—which echo through my head along with the vision of my dad sitting at his "desk," the bedside table in his rehabilitation room—are instructive as I go forward, arranging and rearranging the bits and pieces of my new way of empty-nest living. His inspiration reminds me that our attitude means more than any of our circumstances. Our mindset possesses the awesome power to change the course of our moments, our days, and, yes, our lives.

Lucky for me, I have his example to lead the way. I see him calling his relatives and friends to find out how they're doing. Going out to lunch whenever he gets the chance. Sending notes of appreciation to all those who help make his days brighter. Always showing genuine interest in the lives of those around him. Finding ways to help however he can.

That acceptance of his, that grace of embracing whatever moment he finds himself in, perhaps shared mostly by example, that's Dad's best advice of all.

Taken to heart.

Magic on the Vineyard

This weekend we could drive the fifteen miles or so to Quonset, where we could catch the high-speed catamaran that would jet us to Martha's Vineyard in ninety minutes flat, avoiding the traffic that, especially on Friday afternoons, tends to clog the roads and bridges in Newport and on Cape Cod. We could. But we aren't.

Instead, on this sunny October Friday afternoon—when we're reveling in our newfound freedom—Ernie and I drive the hour and a half to Woods Hole to catch the large old-fashioned car ferry. After boarding, we sit on the deck as the ship slowly pulls away from the dock and heads for the open sea. We're taking this less efficient route for a reason: because at some point during our unhurried journey to the island, somewhere while chugging along through the choppy waters of the Atlantic as the shoreline behind us disappears from view, we know that we're truly getting away, that we're actually leaving the gravity of our busy lives behind, if only for a while.

I look over at my husband as he tugs on the bill of his Red Sox hat, mindful that the breeze has picked up. "How many years have we been coming here?"

"A long time," he says, looking out on the horizon where the ocean stretches as far as we can see. "Our first trip was before we were married."

A boy standing on the bow tosses bits of bread into the air. He's mesmerized by the seagulls that somehow stay in flight right alongside the boat, suspended in midair, grabbing every last bite in their greedy beaks.

"Why do you think we keep coming back?"

"Over the years, the Vineyard has become our favorite retreat, our sanctuary. I think we come to escape when we need to relax and unwind." Ernie looks over at me and smiles. "We've made so many memories here."

True. We've biked all over the island, the pine-scented trails, and the sandy roads along the beaches. We've happened along all kinds of adventures, too. Hearing Walter Cronkite speak at a church in Oak Bluffs. Catching a Livingston Taylor concert in Edgartown.

"Let's not forget the night the Clintons were here with the Secret Service all around, blocking the streets with their SUVs, and the snipers on the rooftops," I say. "How I managed to get into the ice cream shop to meet them, I still don't know."

"I guess I looked too suspicious," Ernie says. "That's why the Secret Service wouldn't let me in."

"You do have that look. Something about your dark eyes," I say with a wink.

Ernie reaches over and takes my hand. "So that, my dear, is why we're heading there to celebrate our anniversary."

We return to our car as the ferry pulls into Vineyard Haven. We drive along the shoreline to Edgartown, our windows open, the salty breeze blowing in our hair, the gulls calling to us. Loud. Louder.

We arrive at our favorite hotel and check in, receiving an unexpected gift when we go to our room. We unlock the door to a spacious one-bedroom luxury suite complete with a living room, fireplace, and a private porch overlooking breathtaking flower gardens. A surprise upgrade from our hotel at no extra charge! Happy anniversary to us!

The magic continues the next day with the Indian summer weather reminding us of another October day, twenty-three years ago, when we formalized our decision to be together. On this Saturday morning, as so often happens when you run your own business, Ernie has a little writing to get out of the way, so I'm free for a few hours to do whatever I want. That finds me lacing up my Sauconys and heading out along the coastline. Something about the change of scenery and the surprisingly warm sunshine inspires me to keep going. And going.

I'm not surprised I'm running farther here without thinking about it. This island seems to hold a special power for us. It's here that we've come up with some of our best ideas, had some of our most profound discussions, and made some of our most important and enduring decisions. There's nothing in the land or sea or sky here that's vastly different from other places we've traveled. Yet we keep coming back.

Maybe you've discovered a getaway like this, too. A place that energizes you, changes your perspective, and helps you feel and think in a deeper way. A destination that draws you back again and again for no other reason than that sense it gives you. That sense of peace, contentment, and limitless possibilities.

There's definitely great energy here. Before too long, I'm approaching the nearby town of Oak Bluffs, a far longer run than intended. By the time I make my way back to the hotel, I've logged thirteen miles, I'm feeling terrific, and it's still morning!

After a shower and breakfast, Ernie and I head out for the day with no particular plan in mind (our favorite vacation mode!). We find ourselves meandering in and out of shops, driving here and there, sipping coffee, talking about our lives and nothing at all, truly enjoying each moment, every one of them, during our time away. As we make our way back into the driveway that leads to the hotel, we notice a crowd of people in suits and dresses gathering for a wedding out on the lawn. In order to direct the guests to the right place, there's a sign posted with a large heart on it pointing the way. Inside the heart are these letters: E & R.

I look over at my husband. "Can you believe that?"

When we get back to our room, Ernie pours two glasses of wine. We find a perfect perch on our porch overlooking the gathering crowd in their floral dresses and handsome suits. We sit there in a state of bliss. What are the odds that on the anniversary of the very day we were married, there would be a wedding at our hotel on the lawn right outside the private porch of our luxury suite, which we did not order or expect, a wedding where the bride and groom just so happen to have the exact same first initials as we do? How cosmic and wonderful. I've got to believe that it's exceptionally good karma for them just starting out on their journey together, and for us, too, who are twenty-three years into what has been, and still is, a magical adventure.

Seeing through New Windows

Spanning three-quarters of the wall from floor to ceiling, there are two new windows facing east in our bedroom. They are the classic kind, double-hung, with six panes on the top. They open easily and wide, unlike the crank-out ones that had been stuck shut for years and years before we finally got around to replacing them.

I like our new windows so much that I convinced Ernie to move our bed to the opposite side of the room for a fresh look, a cozy fit for our new life, just us two. These days we sleep with three small windows just above the head of our bed and the two large ones to our right. In the months since we moved back into our home after the renovation, bedtime has become transformed.

In the quiet moments before drifting off to sleep, we lie there under moonlight and starlight, the shadows of the day scuttling by with the clouds. On stormy nights, we huddle in the darkness, the rain hammering above our heads, the wind howling all around as we pull the blankets higher, tighter. When it's warmer, we fling the windows wide open and allow the breeze to gently brush across our faces, fresh air filling our lungs as we drift away.

It's as if the world has opened up before our eyes. On the weekends, if we linger long enough, we awaken to the magenta-scarlet spectacle in the east pushing away the night's dark curtain. Since our sleigh bed has moved to its new perch, we've seen green leaves turn to blazes before reluctantly letting go of their branches only to nestle into the gutters or rustle down to the lawn below. We've caught glimpses of deer foraging in the yard, squirrels scampering on the oaks, crimson cardinals flitting in and out of our frame. In the darkness of winter, we've watched snow blanket our roof until it eventually slip-slides down onto the new deck that's waiting there for us when the warmer months come back around.

The new windows have even inspired a new idea. Sometimes in the morning, I slip downstairs in my pajamas, brew coffee, grab my workbag, and then tuck myself back into bed. There I sit, propped up on pillows, my mug sitting on what I now refer to as my morning stand. As the clouds part for the sun, I pull my favorite books from my bag to begin my morning with a little inspiration, then move to my laptop to begin writing. Today's topic? Our new windows.

The ironic thing is that we've lived here for more than two decades. This is the house we came home to after we were married. We raised Geoff and Meredith here, and Lizzie, too. We've hosted many gatherings here: family, friends, and even Denise and Claude's wedding. But it's taken me all this time to see it through a fresh lens.

The sculptor Frederick Franck once said, "Merely looking at the world around us is immensely different from seeing it." His point is well taken.

Merely looking at the world equates to a drive-by existence in which we're careening at top speed from one task to the next with our heads down, our eyes riveted on the road ahead. There are no detours, no U-turns, and no stops allowed. But when we open our eyes, when we truly open our eyes wide and see, we're opening our minds to a newfound appreciation for all that surrounds us. We're letting gratitude flood in for all the gifts in our lives, for the very gift *of* our lives. Nothing that comes into our vision can be taken for granted any longer.

How many times have Ernie and I wrestled with the decision of whether to move to another town, a bigger house, or a cottage by the sea? How many plans did we consider and reconsider to buy land, to design and build a place we could only imagine? How many dreams and schemes came and went before we finally asked ourselves what mattered most, rolled up our sleeves, and turned the house that had sheltered us for all those years into a home we could love for many more?

Two new windows have opened a whole new world for us. I call them my grateful windows. Because everything I'm the most thankful for in my life has been here all along. It just took me a while to see.

The Long Run

Ever since Meredith attended grade school in Newport, I've enjoyed running up and down the historic streets there, especially the shady paths near Bellevue Avenue with its Gilded Age mansions and echoes from the past. So many times, I've thought of taking the wide turn out onto Ocean Drive, putting one foot in front of the other, and taking the long scenic loop along the coastline like I used to do during my marathon training days. So many times, I've told myself I could do it, but because of an errand, meeting, or appointment, I couldn't. Or, for just plain lack of energy or motivation, I didn't. But one of these days, I promised myself, I'd take that turn.

Maybe today.

I start out slowly at first, jogging down America's Cup Avenue. It's early, but the bright morning has coaxed quite a few people out of bed. Cars rumble by on the cobblestone streets. All around me, walkers are walking, strollers are strolling, bikers are biking, and more than a few runners are already out here hitting the pavement.

My thoughts swirl, blowing this way and that like the sand my Sauconys kick up along the road. At this moment, only one thing is clear. I must run. One way or another, I'm going to put some mileage in today, no matter what. I'm going to work out some things in my head, one mile at a time.

For some reason, the stress has been getting to me lately. Meredith's anxiety is spiking, and so are the frequency and length of her calls. I know she gets like this. I know she's learning to calm and center herself, finding balance on her own. But sometimes, when things spiral too far out of control, she needs a familiar voice to give her a push in the right direction.

The more I stretch as a mother, the more I miss my own. I see her almost everywhere I go and in almost everything I do. I hear her calm voice in my ears. I feel her steady hand on mine, guiding and inspiring me every day. Why is life like this? Why is change so abrupt and final? Why do we see things so clearly in hindsight when it would have been better to have a little more realization and gratitude in the moment for all that is given to us?

So here I am, the accidental matriarch, trying to take care of our family. My father, with his high-flying spirit, recently ran into some health issues that threatened to slow him down. His heart needed a valve replacement. We got him through. His shoulder was injured by a misguided pneumonia shot. We got him through. He fell in the middle of the night and fractured a bone in his hip. We got him through. And we'll get him through again.

Denise feels the strain, too. She's commuting all over the state for work. She and Claude are renovating their house while living in the mess that such an ambitious project necessitates while still trying to carve out some sense of joy and beauty in their lives. Sometimes, when I get weak and wobbly, I want to lean on her. But I know she needs to lean on me, too.

There's the turn up ahead. *Take it*, I tell myself. *Take it now!* But Ocean Drive is so long. But I've come so far. Back and forth. Back and forth. And then it's here. The turn. And just like that, I decide. This is the day.

Look over there. King Park with its strip of rocky beach. I used to go there with my best buddy, Carol, when we were little. I recall a little store across the street where we'd stop for something to eat. "Do I have slimy green stuff in my teeth?" she'd ask me, pointing to her shiny smile and her perfect rows of pearly white teeth.

"No," I'd report.

"Well, *you* do!" she'd say, and we'd burst into uncontrollable laughter as I worked the telltale lettuce from my sandwich out from between my teeth.

The odd thing about this route is that, in recent times, I've only driven it by car. But today, on foot, the memory of the passing scenery is so very different. It seems a long way to Fort Adams, but I eventually get there and go past the entrance, past the rocky cliffs and paths where my friend Sharon and I once brought our pack of kids and dogs for an adventure. I remember the dogs running free, splashing in and out of the water to the delight of our kids. And the kids within us, too.

The miles go by one after the next. Finally, I make my way out to where the road borders the open ocean. The breeze is nice and, at this point, so welcome. The view of the waves crashing in on the rocks is breathtaking. I'm surprised by the throng of people out here at this early hour. An older couple holding hands. A few guys flying kites. And then I come to the very spot where my friend from work, Jack, happened upon me one day when I was struggling with a long run while training for my first marathon. This was the point where I couldn't make it any further, way out on Ocean Drive in the middle of nowhere. Why on earth did he show up at that very moment? I have no idea. Perhaps a guardian angel was looking out for me and sent Jack to get me going again during a dark time when, all in one summer, I got hit by a truck that careened up onto the curb where I was standing, struggled through a painful divorce, and lost my job.

I never fully understood the healing power of running back then.
I do now.

There's Gooseberry Beach on my right. So many memories come
flooding back. The early mornings, when I got up with Dad and we
peddled our bikes all this way in the dawning hours. The shore where
I brought my curly red-haired toddler, and Geoff loved it so much
that it was all I could do to get him on the seat on the back of my bike
for the ride home. Along the way, I felt his weight list over to one side,
my little passenger, tired, content, and sound asleep.

I remember, too, the day Ernie and I stayed here so long we didn't
notice the sun slipping down, the people packing up their towels
and umbrellas, the cars driving away, until we got to the parking
lot and discovered the gate was locked and we had no way out. If it
hadn't been for a lifeguard returning to fetch a forgotten backpack,
we might have had to spend the night.

Aaargh! I remember this hill, too. The long, torturous climb after
swimming lessons at Girl Scout camp, the salt sticking to my skin,
the rubber bathing cap that split the ends of my long hair. The same
camp where I enrolled Meredith many summers later so she could
climb that same long hill after a long day of swimming, much to her
chagrin.

And here's the rocky inlet where I took her when she was in pre-
school, my little bookworm who needed some fresh air. She was telling me a story, as I recall, her arms waving in the air as she described
the fairies that swam too far out to sea and how they were rescued, just
as a lone seagull swooped down and nabbed the chocolate chip muffin
out of her small hands before she could even take a bite. Vallamose,
we named him, soon to become the villain in her next story.

Finally, I take the turn off Ocean Drive and head to Bellevue
Avenue. I pass by Rovensky Park where, many years ago, I stopped

to sit on the stone wall with my swollen belly, ten days overdue. I had been out for a walk and suddenly suffered cramps that I didn't realize were labor pains. What was I thinking, walking a mile away from home all alone? As it turned out, that ended up being the night when I made it to the hospital just in the nick of time to welcome Geoff into the world.

Another few minutes, and I'm back to where I began. I made it. I've come full circle. What a silly thought I had been entertaining for these past few years. All this back-to-me stuff. In some ways, it's true that I'm reclaiming more of my life for me. I've got more freedom now, more time on my hands, more flexibility in my schedule. But when I became pregnant the first time, I changed in a way I could never have foreseen. A good way. A forever way. As my kids grew up, I did, too, leaving behind the selfishness and egotism of my younger days. Things I thought I knew, I didn't. Things I thought were important, weren't. Things I thought didn't matter were all that did.

If I were to take this moment in time to design a life that revolved around me alone, my existence would quickly become as empty as a drum. What I've come to truly appreciate is that my marriage, my children, my family, my friends, my community—these are the gifts in life that mean the most. And I now understand that in a life surrounded by people I love, there's bound to be adversity, the inevitable ups and downs. It would be naive to think otherwise, to believe that somehow my kids' departure would usher in a Valhalla-like existence, an endless country-club vacation. That would be nice. And hopefully, there will be long, relatively carefree stretches on the road ahead. Believe me, I'm looking forward to them! But what I've come to realize is that stress and hardship and change are invitations to grow, opportunities to rise to the occasion. And learning to embrace love and simple pleasures can bring profound joy to a grateful heart.

Who knows how our lives will turn out? Who can say what twist or which turn could be right around the corner? Who can ever know? What I do know, right here and right now, is that I am moving, and I am breathing, remembering the road I've been on, and paving a new one as I go along.

And I am strong.

Strong enough for the long run.

Acknowledgements

There's no way this memoir or the newspaper column that preceded it could have come about without bringing to light some private moments in the lives of my family and friends. No two people were more affected than my children, Geoffrey Brownell and Meredith Lussier-Schenck, who grew up during the years of my column and left home in the pages of this book (they assure me the leaving had nothing to do with the writing). My parents, Elaine and André Lussier, were always enthusiastic supporters of whatever I wanted to write and, for that matter, whatever I wanted to do. Thankfully, my sister Denise Lussier and her husband Claude Verdier, feel the same way. My husband Ernie Schenck has always been a steadfast believer in my writing and in me. Here in the nest we created together, we're happily discovering—and much to our surprise—it's anything but empty.

My gratitude extends to all those who've helped make this book a reality and improved it along the way. Thank you to Jacquelyn Mitchard for her challenge to go deeper with my writing and her artful editing, to Brooke Warner for her structural suggestions and warm welcome to She Writes Press, to all the talented people there including Julie Metz and Addison Gallegos, to Signe Jorgensen for her insightful copy editing, to Joan McElroy for her sharp-eyed proof-reading, to my sister She Write Press authors for their camaraderie and support, to PR by the Book especially Marika Flatt and Debbie Lykins for their expertise and enthusiasm, and to my son Geoff and Dan Carey for their marketing and social media smarts and guidance.

I'd also like to thank Joel Rawson, Executive Editor of *The Providence Journal* at the time, for green lighting my column and the many readers who encouraged me and shared moments of their own lives. It's through our stories, after all, that we come to know we're not alone.

About the Author

photo credit: Ernie Schenck

Rita Lussier is an award-winning journalist and writer whose column "For the Moment" was a popular feature of *The Providence Journal* for 12 years. Her writing has also been featured on National Public Radio, in *The Boston Globe*, *The New York Daily News* and many online publications. Recently, she won first place for her human-interest story in the 2022 Erma Bombeck Writing Competition, an honor she has received three times.

Rita coaches writers and has worked as a publicist and editor. She has taught at both the University of Rhode Island and Rhode Island College. Her educational credentials include a master's degree from the Medill School of Journalism at Northwestern University. She lives with her husband in Jamestown, Rhode Island where she enjoys running, walking, and spending time with family and friends.

Looking for your next great read?

We can help!

Visit www.shewritespress.com/next-read
or scan the QR code below for a list
of our recommended titles.

She Writes Press is an award-winning
independent publishing company founded to
serve women writers everywhere.